COUNTRY SCHOOL, FISHING AND A DOG;

THE SEASONS OF LIFE ON A FAMILY FARM AS I RECOLLECT

J.D. SCHERE

authorHOUSE™

1663 LIBERTY DRIVE, SUITE 200
BLOOMINGTON, INDIANA 47403
(800) 839-8640
WWW.AUTHORHOUSE.COM

First published by AuthorHouse 04/14/05

ISBN: 1-4208-4062-2 (sc)
ISBN: 1-4208-4063-0 (dj)

Library of Congress Control Number: 2005902274

Printed in the United States of America
Bloomington, Indiana

This book is printed on acid-free paper.

For my daughters Jayme and Sabrina, who loved to hear the stories of life on the farm. For my wife Melissa, who still has to listen to the stories. And to my Mom, Dad and my two sisters, I hope you will understand how important you are to me as you recall those days on the farm.

CHAPTER ONE
REMEMBERING THE FARM

*"Be careful to always remember where you
came from; otherwise, you will never achieve
that place of destiny that you were born on this
earth to occupy."—Grandpa Pharmacist*

"Dang it, I left the light on in the barn again," said my dad as he came in from another day of hard work. "Would you mind going out and shutting it off for me?" he said looking in my direction.

Of course I wouldn't mind, but I had to make sure which light it was that he left on. "You mean that light that screws in the socket right over the top of the work bench?"

"Yep," said my dad as he sat down to pull off his boots.

As I left the kitchen heading outside, I began to plan in my mind how I was going to reach that darn light. It had been installed by my dad so that he would have more light over the top of the workbench, it had been installed without the convenience of a light switch, it had been installed in a manner that meant you had to be able to spin the bulb, the bulb that was always hot, counterclockwise with your fingers until it went out.

Now, this would not be a problem for an adult with a pair of gloves on, but for me it presented multiple challenges. First of all, I was only a few inches taller than the top of the work bench, and the light was a good two foot higher up from the top of that bench. This meant I had to climb up on the bench then maintain my balance while trying to unscrew the bulb from the light socket.

Of course, climbing up on top of the bench was no problem, and on this day I was once again under the impression that my hands had a layer of asbestos on them, as I tried to unscrew the bulb with my bare hands.

Just as I was reaching for the bulb, my dog, Yogi, came sauntering into the barn. He sat down right in front of the workbench and looked up at me with his "you know that this is only going to lead to trouble" kinda look. Of course, he was right.

Balancing myself on top of the workbench, I reached up for the light, which by now must have been about one thousand degrees, as it had been on for a few hours, and of course, was burned on all five of my fingers when I grabbed the bulb.

As the pain raced from my fingertips to my brain, I lost my balance on the workbench and began a slow, guided descent, backside first, towards the dirt floor of our barn.

Yogi, my faithful dog that was always looking out for my best interests, began to bark furiously a warning that when translated said, "Watch out for the board with the nail sticking out of it!" But of course, he should have been there when I first came into the barn, 'cause I hadn't noticed the board, or the nail, which was now making its existence known to me by poking its pointed tip into my rear end, right square in the middle of my right cheek.

Sitting on the floor of the barn, still in shock from the fall, I began to wonder why my faithful companion's barking had turned from a bark of warning to the unmistakable bark of hilarity. Then I began to experience the first feelings of pain generated by this nail that had tacked its accompanying chunk of wood onto my rear end.

My yelling and the dog's barking got the attention of my sisters, who just happened to be sitting on the front porch of the house. They came running out to the barn to see what was up and immediately joined my dog in fits of barking laughter at the sight of me standing there with a two-by-four stuck to my rear end.

"Don't worry, Johnny, we will get it off!" they assured me as one of them held me while the other one pulled on the board. The removal of the board revealed the nail, sending both sisters and dog into another panicked fit of laughter.

"You had this nail stuck in your butt!" stated my older sister as she wiped the tears from her eyes.

My older sister, ever the analyst, grabbed the board from the even older sister to evaluate the nail and explained, "Look, this nail is rusty and it went into your butt. Now you're going to get lockjaw and die!"

I had been relatively calm up to this point, but hearing the sister that I trusted most telling me that I was going to get lockjaw and die was all it took for me to lose my composure, and the four of us set off for the house seeking the wisdom of Mom and Dad. Would I live? Was I going to die? So many questions, so few answers. Then my dog, Yogi, suddenly looked at me and said, "John, this job is a pain in the butt! If I have to work with these people any longer, I am going to quit!"

Startled by the fact that my dog was actually talking to me, I suddenly realized that I was not on our family farm but sitting in a office, wearing a suit and tie, with a frustrated-looking woman standing in front of the desk apparently seeking my counsel with regard to some issues she was having with those she was supposed to be supervising!

I could still feel the pain from that nail that introduced itself to my rear end on a day that occurred nearly forty years ago. But the pain was there like this event had just occurred. What was up with that?

My office door was usually open. Open, as I wanted the people that I worked with to feel that they could come in to talk whenever they wanted to. While I didn't agree with all of the current-day management philosophies, I did believe that a manager should be easily accessible to those that they are supposed to be managing. The reality of it was that I really do enjoy talking with people.

I had begun to notice that I was spending more and more time daydreaming about those years I had spent growing up on our family's Midwestern farm. Not that it is a bad thing to be reliving memories, but I found that I was doing this when people that I cared about were standing in front of me seeking counsel on issues that were causing them stress.

I really knew that something was not right when one day I stopped being able to understand what it was that these team members were saying. They would come into my office and begin speaking, but all I could hear was, "Blah, blah, blah, blah, blah."

I was beginning to understand that before long I was going to have to cope with the reality that these periods of daydreaming were being triggered by a desire that was growing inside me to be someplace other than where I was.

Now you need to understand that I had inherited some tendencies that would classify me as being thickheaded, stubborn, mule-headed, even a control freak. And though I couldn't prove it, it seemed to me that my body was using these daydreams as an act of defense against those negative thoughts I was having that were counterproductive to my positive existence.

Was it possible that my own body was trying to tell me that it was time for me to exist someplace else?

I even entertained, for a brief moment, the thought of applying for a federal grant to conduct research on my daydreaming. After all, this topic seemed no less absurd than some other phenomena I have read that the government granted research money for.

Then the reality of this all slapped my face with the same impact of that nail-bearing two-by-four years ago!

I realized that I had reached a point in my life in which I was losing interest in being paid to do something I no longer had a passion to do. Listening to people whine and complain was taking me into a state of daydreaming as a defense mechanism to prevent me from becoming callous towards good people.

None of us likes to have our day ruined. None of us really enjoys being subjected to a continuous barrage of conflict. No matter what your environment, no matter how it is that you get to that point where you can't function in the manner you are accustomed to, the human mind has the ability take us away from a chaotic environment without us even having to leave the room.

For me, my mind was transporting me back to a place in my memory that stored adventures from a time in my life when everything was new and exciting: the years of my youth spent on the family farm. The present realities of today were being preempted with adventures from a time when life was really good.

Now, I don't want to mislead you into thinking that growing up on the farm didn't create its own types of stress. As you will see, there was plenty of good soil in which stress could spread its roots. But when you're a kid and discovery awaits at the beginning of each day, you had no time for stress and anxiety. Those were feelings and experiences that were better left for the adults to deal with.

The freedom that was experienced growing up on the farm was being recalled by my mind whenever my own instincts where being suppressed by a corporately imposed prison of responses.

The right things to say and do that had been taught to me in the classrooms of growing up on the farm were no longer considered appropriate in today's world.

I remember my grandfather, the one that was a pharmacist, telling me something that I was now beginning to understand. He said, "Be careful to always remember where you came from; otherwise, you will never achieve that place of destiny that you were born on this earth to occupy."

This daydreaming about the farm was a reminder that I had forgotten about who I was and where I had come from. That the road I was on was fast becoming a road that was taking me further and further away from that place where I was suppose to be.

Life on the farm was a marathon of endless hours of work, but it was work that created a marathon of memories. Memories enhanced by the expressions I can still see painted on the remembered faces of those who taught me that work was one of God's blessings.

Living on the farm was a life in which perseverance was the necessary ingredient in order to finish those hours of endless work. Work that, once done, left you with a feeling of goodness. The kind of goodness that gives your mind cause for memories that would later in life fill your daydreams when your soul ached for freedom and new adventure.

Those years lived on the farm were lived in a time when the news wasn't spun but reported. They were lived in a time when the most important economic indicators were simple things that always made sense, like the number of bushels per acre, cattle and hog prices by the hundredweight, or the cost of grain per bushel.

It was a time when none of these indicators were more important than that of a man's word. Yes meant yes, and no meant no! Work ethic was more important than a college degree.

It was a place in time when the lifestyle dictated that when you worked, you worked hard, but when you played, you also played hard.

Life on the farm was a stage for learning about all the good things that made up life on this earth. The farm provided a stage on which you learned how to deal with the not so good things that happen in life as well as how to enjoy the mostly good things that occurred.

Years later, sitting in my office in a state of daydreaming, it occurred to me that I was learning a lesson that I am certain we all learn sooner or later. The lesson that teaches us that you only learn how important something is to you when you no longer have it!

Life on the farm was one of those jewels that I did not appreciate until it was gone.

It was, and in the confines of my mind still is, the way life was meant to be lived.

Chapter Two
Yogi

"It really doesn't matter much where you are going if you don't have any idea where you are at!"—Grandpa Farmer

I would venture that most of us would understand that you learn different lessons about life while growing up on a farm than you would learn when growing up in a city or in a small town. I would also venture that we would also all agree that most of the lessons we learned have invariably gotten lost somewhere in the fast-paced chaos that makes up our life.

I think that a lot of what I learned got lost in those years spent in high school and college.

I say that lessons got lost in those fast-paced years because it seems that gaining knowledge was a secondary goal of high school and college. Other forces seemed to be in control of those years, forces that can be left for others to write about. I came to the conclusion long ago that growing up had very little to do with going to high school and college.

Growing up is certainly a process that is affected by the conditions created by the environment that you are growing up in. I would guess that the conditions that best lend to the process of growing up are nearly impossible to produce. I am not sure that any of us can say that our high school and college experience had anything to do with actually growing up properly.

Somewhere in my forties, which is considered by some to be an era where you are old enough to know better but by others to be an age in which you are still in the process of growing up, I was spending time searching the far horizon for a clue that would point me in the direction that I should go in, when it suddenly occurred to me that I had no idea where I was.

I remembered being told by my grandpa, the one that was a farmer, "It really doesn't matter much where you are going if you don't have any idea where you are at!"

Now, when you realize that you don't know where you are, you sometimes begin to panic. The anxiety that was being developed in thoughts was being directed by those gangs named hopelessness and despair. These guys began to obscure my own vision of my future, but suddenly my eyes seemed to regain their focus to that 20/20 vision that we always seem to obtain when we reach that point where we have hindsight.

This particular hindsight was suggesting to me that somewhere, probably in that high school mess, I had really missed the narrow path I had been destined to take!

Not only had I missed the path but the ship had sailed without me, the compass had long ago lost its magnetic north, and those dreams I had always dreamed of had been preempted with reruns of *The Twilight Zone.*

As my thoughts slowly made an about-face, searching for a clue, I was clearly taken back to the moment in time that contained my eighth birthday party.

I suppose that we can all trace our lives back to a point in time that we could say was the exact moment in our life when we blew right by the opportunity of becoming an exceptional story and became instead just another statistic of average existence.

Was it possible that I was being shown that exact moment in my life when I passed by fame and fortune? Or was I only being reminded of the one birthday in my life that was not accompanied by the traditional birthday gift?

My eighth birthday party was the one when I was given a gift that kept on giving for years to come. It was a gift that I unwrapped in the middle of the old granary located in the south end of the barn on our farm.

Our farm's barn could be spotted by the knowing traveler's eye as he drove down the main highway that ran east to west not two miles west of our farm.

Not more than ten to fifteen travelers could have been driving down the highway at this precise moment in time, and none of them could have understood the significance of what was going on in our barn. They were as clueless as I was to the significance of the gift I was being given, a gift given without the usual cake and ice cream accompaniment, a gift wrapped in a not-so-carefully-tied-shut burlap bag.

I remember paying no attention to the fact that the gunny sack was a little bit wet. It really didn't make any difference to me, as I was totally focused on what was inside the wet bag.

I remember the anticipation of my parents as they stood there in the doorway of that granary, awaiting the excitement that would be released by the opening of that wet, burlap bag. Was it possible that my parents already understood the importance of this day, and this present, and the profound effect it would have on the rest of my life?

It would be many years later before I would fully appreciate just how important that particular birthday was when held up next to those many other birthdays that I would celebrate. For on this day, exploding from that wet gunny sack and standing on shaky and shivering legs was hope for my future, the catalyst for many years of discovery and opportunity, a puppy that we would name Yogi.

Yogi was part collie, part German shepherd, part human being. His pedigree was untraceable. Yogi was the runt of a rather large litter of puppies that was delivered on one of the neighbors' farms. I'm not sure about all the details that led to how my parents obtained him; all I know is that my parents brought him home on this day and gave him to me.

Yogi got his name as the result of my sisters calling out the names of those cartoon characters that we faithfully watched each Saturday morning. When my older sister called out the name Yogi, his little ears stood straight up and he proceeded to rumble and stumble right into my lap.

Thus was the beginning of many years of mostly unplanned, spontaneous adventures.

You see, though I did not realize it at the time, Yogi had a real knack for getting me into trouble. His was a knack that created adventures so incredible that years later when I regaled them to anyone that would listen, the listener would usually adorn his face with a look of disbelief and walk away muttering words like, "Yeah, sure."

Yogi grew up to be a dog that weight almost eighty pounds. When he stood on his back legs his paws would reach the chest of my six-foot-four-inch dad. And Yogi was always ready for something, anything!

He would jump into the back of the pickup truck and sit there and wait for hours. Because in his world you never knew when the pickup would start up and go somewhere.

Yogi loved riding in the pickup. When riding in the back of the pickup he would proclaim his joy for all the world to hear, and his barking would carry for miles.

When things didn't go so well, Yogi had instincts that told him exactly when to shut up, say nothing, and just cuddle up next to you. He would put that big head of his on your lap and look at you with his big eyes with a compassion that would permeate into the worst of days.

He would always be happy to see you; I don't think I ever saw Yogi ignore anyone.

Yogi had a knack for teaching me all about friendship, love, compassion, selflessness, and on one particular day, he taught me a lesson about Lordship.

It seems that God can use people, places, and even dogs to teach us about the mysteries of His deep love for us. He can even use the memory of a dog that has not been a physical part of your life for a number of years.

Yogi had died some thirty years before that day when I was reading a parable of Christ taught in the Bible in Mathew 15:22-28. In my search to understand what I was reading, that Spirit that God placed in me suddenly transformed me past the throes of wonderment regarding the what-ifs ... the maybes ... and the if-I-had-onlys ... in my life, to a place that I now know to be a place that is best described as in the Peace of Christ.

As only a loving God can do, my mind was anchored to a mental picture of the dog mentioned in the parable I was reading, who was eating the crumbs from his master's table. Then my mind projected back to the simpler days of my own life, to the memories of my own dog, Yogi, joyfully licking up the crumbs that fell from those fresh-baked cookies that my mom gave me when I was a kid.

It was a memory that had been skillfully programmed into my mind by The Creator, who knew all along about this road that I would be traveling down. The Creator who has known since before the earth was formed that I would reach this point in the journey of my life, when the memories of a loving relationship with a dog named Yogi would be the key I would need to unlock some mysteries that my own insecurities had created.

It was a memory that would remind me that I at one time had possessed enough faith to turn a dog into my best friend. It was a memory that would help me to understand the endless rewards that would come from an even smaller amount of faith needed to make Jesus my best friend, which would then allow The Holy Spirit to help me realize the full life desired for us all by a living and loving God!

Chapter Three
The Seasons: Summer

"Share your candy with your sisters; show
them that you love them."—Mom

Growing up on the farm played a big part in the development of the character traits, attitudes, and personalities that governed the expectations I had about the role I would play in this world. People were involved in a lot of these lessons, but it was Yogi that taught me about what can be done with a positive and upbeat attitude.

It seemed that he was always upbeat and his attitude was driven by joy. His enthusiasm was endless. There was always something important to do.

I have watched today's kids as they struggle to find something to do when there is nothing that interests them on television or they are tired of playing the video games they have played over and over. When these kids are asked to use their imagination and create something to do, they simply place a look of indifference upon their own ability to think and return to surfing the cable networks or Internet.

I suppose that had I been raised in their world, I too could have been seduced by the television or by the video games and Internet websites that kids seem to enjoy so much.

While I don't now recall having those moments when I would long for something exciting to do, I am sure that they did exist, and I am equally sure that those moments did not last long, as it seems that life on the farm had a way of supercharging a kid's imagination.

Of course, what you could do and couldn't do was impacted by the changing seasons of the year. On the Midwestern farm the seasons of the year dictated the events that made up the routine of each day.

In the summer, you would swear that time slowed way down to the point that the clocks would actually stop right in the midst of the heat of the day. Of course, that extension of time just provided a kid with more opportunities for adventure provided the adults had not already overbooked your day with the multitude of summer chores that they seemed to be able to create.

One activity that provided entertainment on hot summer afternoons was watching the antics of chickens, like when they discovered our garden. Not a small feat for a chicken, as the area where the garden was located must have appeared to a chicken to be miles away from their home, the chicken coop.

It was real live entertainment to watch the adventurous chickens that dared to get within the invisible confines that surrounded the family's garden plot. The dance of a chicken as it scratches the ground to dig up its daily bread in the form of worms, bugs, and seeds can be highly entertaining to a curious farm kid.

Each summer the family garden also provided an opportunity to earn extra money. In fact, the first money I ever earned came from an agreement that I made with my grandpa that earned me a nickel for every group of ten potato bugs I plucked off of the leaves of the potato plants.

Fifty potato bugs yielded enough money for a farm kid to go into the local five-and-dime store in town to purchase more candy than you could eat in a week. Candy that generally didn't last the week, as those lazy sisters of mine, who wouldn't think of touching a bug, would always come begging for candy.

It was begging that seemed to always end with an admonishment from our mom that sounded something like, "Share your candy with your sisters; show them that you love them." As if love had anything at all to do with the consumption of candy bought with money earned by your own sweat and toil.

I remember the excitement of that summer day when my dad finally uttered those long awaited words, "It's time for you to learn how to drive a tractor." Excitement that too soon turned to agony when, after becoming proficient enough at using the endless number of gears that grow within a tractor, I was promoted to the tasks of cultivating corn, raking hay, and spraying weeds.

The worst of these tasks was without a doubt the process of cultivating corn.

I didn't realize just how long a corn row could be until I had sat behind the wheel of the tractor dragging a cultivator around the cornfield. It was then that I was led to believe that the corn rows on our family farm had to be at least seven miles long.

You see, cultivating corn is a discipline that requires that you do not drive any faster than somewhere around one mile per hour. Drive too fast and you bury the young corn plants with the dirt thrown by the shovels mounted on the back of the cultivator. Drive too slow and the weeds next to the young plants will not be covered up enough to prevent them from growing as fast as the corn, because not enough dirt will be thrown by the shovels to shield them from the life-providing light of the sun.

You had to find the perfect speed, a speed comparable to that of a turtle racing at top speed on an uphill highway. Of course, when you found the perfect speed for cultivating, it was always that same speed that would foster the perfect environment for the breeding of the cultivator's most dreaded malady: boredom!

I don't believe that the human mind is capable of producing enough ideas, dreams, or songs remembered with which you could combat the noisy drone created by a tractor as it speeds along at less than one mile an hour through a hundred acres of baby corn plants. You would long for the excitement found at the end of each row, when you were allowed to show your deft ability to maneuver your tractor one hundred and eighty degrees in a performance of precision that would place your tractor precisely in the middle of the next four rows of corn that needed cultivating.

It was a skill that came about with much practice, much development of coordination between the eyes, the arms and hands, the feet and the brakes, and the throttle on the tractor. It seemed that my dad always planted the corn too close to the fence that was always located at the end of each row. Not just any fence: it was a barbed-wire fence with the four strands of wire that required repair every time I had the privilege of being the cultivator.

I remember the time that I fell asleep at the wheel of the tractor, taking out hundreds of innocent corn plants in the middle the field we called our bottom forty. I remember thinking that no one would ever know only to be found out during the summer irrigation season that always followed the cultivating season of the corn.

You see, when it came time to irrigate that particular section of the lower forty, the irrigation water seemed to disappear, never making it from the siphon tubes placed to pump the water down the rows out of the irrigation ditch on the west side of the field to the end of those eight rows on the east side of the field. I remember the grumbling from my dad as each of us with a shovel over our shoulder headed into the field of shoulder-high dew-covered corn in search of why the water was mysteriously not making its appointment with the east.

When we finally came upon that barren spot in the middle of the field, devoid of corn, rows crisscrossing over each other in a manner that I suggested was consistent with the behavior reportedly associated with little green men in spaceships, my dad went to work repairing the damage with a look of all-knowing understanding planted upon his face.

I am sure that my dad often thought he would have been better off leaving me to chasing chickens or pigs each time he set foot into the depths of the cornfield in search of the missing irrigation water, knowing full well that he would certainly discover the results of those unscheduled naps I had taken while at the wheel of the cultivating tractor.

Chapter Four
The Seasons: Fall

"Well now, that wasn't quite so bad."—Yogi

The fall season brought with it the family's reward for all the summer's hard work. The harvest was always more exciting due to the fact that you didn't know how much time you had to get everything out of the field, as Mother Nature was terribly unpredictable. Each year the race was on to get the corn out of the field before first snow; and the tomatoes, beans, and potatoes had to be canned, frozen, or sacked and placed into the cellar before the first frost. The hay had to be transported from the hayfields into the big area saved for their winter residence east of the barn. It was a space left to the tall weeds of a wet summer that would become home to a small population of haystacks when the temperatures began to drop each fall.

I am certain that any farm kid could write a book about the endless hours of adventure created by a haystack. Whether they were in groups or standing by themselves out in the middle of a field, haystacks added an identity to the countryside that has long been lost to the technological advances of bailers, choppers, and alfalfa pellets.

Every fall on our farm, each stack of hay was moved from its peaceful isolation out in the hayfield, and it became an integral inhabitant of the city of haystacks we put together each fall for the express enjoyment of Yogi and me. These haystack cities were far better than any of the rock gyms kids flock to nowadays.

There was an individual style and art form developed by each individual while jumping from stack to stack. I never understood how the sport of haystack jumping did not become a part of the Olympics. In my mind, I was a world-class haystack jumper, developing a number of dramatic styles used in leaping from stack to stack.

I must also mention the great care and precision thoughtfully given by the creator of each of those stacks of hay. City folk would take long, carefully planned Sunday afternoon trips into the countryside for the sole purpose of admiring the artistic beauty of the haystack. Some farmers were well known for their specific artistic flair that you would see only when viewing those haystacks that occupied their personal farm's hay flats.

My dad was more into the non-structured, non-symmetrical aspects of hay stacking. His stacks were longer and wider than most. The reason he gave for this style was that he would then have fewer stacks to move into the farmyard come fall.

He had a similar philosophy about why his corn rows were so crooked. "You can get more corn in the row than when they are straight," he would always explain.

I remember one particular fall when we began the process of moving hay from the alfalfa field located just to the south of our farmhouse. It was a hayfield that I had special interest in on this particular year, for you see, that doggone dog of mine, Yogi, had convinced me that we needed to turn one of the larger haystacks in this particular field into a clubhouse. He also convinced me that I would need help, so I recruited one of my sisters to help us in the transformation of this haystack into a clubhouse.

We ended up with a wonderful clubhouse, complete with a main lodge room that was hollowed out right in the middle of the haystack. There was a chute, or slide, that provided you the opportunity to seek the safety of the main lodge room from the top of the haystack; you know, for when the parents started hollering for you because they had created some work for you to do.

We even had a maze that encircled the outer perimeter of the haystack.

Of course, being a novice of haystack engineering, I was not certain of the consequences that would occur when a farmer rammed a two-ton hay mover into the underside of the haystack that had been converted into a clubhouse.

This particular fall, when that particular haystack's turn came to be moved into the hay yard, Yogi and I made certain that we had front-row seats for the show. My sister, of course, was not as curious, and her absence was clearly noted.

As the big hay-moving machinery was positioned to take the clubhouse haystack up onto its main bed, Yogi turned coward and hid behind my legs, whining a pathetic moan, turning his head from side to side as the hay mover rammed underneath the rather large haystack.

When the dust had cleared and the profound words of astonishment ceased to flow from my dad's lips, I opened my eyes to witness the results of our undermining of this proud hay structure's carefully planned foundation.

There was the hay mover with one third of the haystack firmly in the middle of the main bed, and the remaining two thirds equally proportioned to the left and right sides of the hay mover's steel resolve. I saw a magnificent, proud pile of hay that seemed to be making one last stand for its right to maintain its isolated existence in the field in which it was formed. The hay draped over the sides of the hay mover, forming a bond with the earth that seemed to be unbreakable.

Yogi came out from behind me, with that wonderful smile he always seemed a have, tongue hanging out to the side, confidence beaming in his face, looking at me as if to say, "Well now, that wasn't quite so bad."

My dad's expression was quite different. He stood there staring at the mess of hay, cap in hand, scratching his head, then looked over to me and said, "I don't suppose you would have any idea how this could happen?" before climbing back on the tractor and moving on to the next haystack.

I was amazed that this adventure into haystack redevelopment, which Yogi and I maintained we were coerced into by a suspiciously absent sister, did not result in one of my dad's progressive discipline plans. Maybe he had a better understanding of farm kid logic than I gave him credit for!

CHAPTER FIVE
THE SEASONS: WINTER

"Those weathermen don't know shit from shinola!"—Grandpa Farmer

Winter provided the best opportunity for me to make amends for all those things that Yogi had talked me into during the year, what with all the holidays that come along with the winter months: Thanksgiving, Christmas, and New Year's.

With each holiday came the gatherings with family so the adults could discuss things related to weather, farm prices, and gossip. The kids discussed which of us had gotten the better of the adults in the year past: both at home and at school.

Best about the winter season were those bonus holidays that accompanied winter snowstorms prompting the closing of all roads and therefore all schools.

I don't believe that anyone fortunate enough to grow up on a farm could have an unfavorable thought about the tranquil silence that comes with a winter storm that dumps a lot of snow on the land you are living on: the peaceful serenity along with the beauty of the snow-laden ground, accompanied by the elegance of the frosted trees when you first set eyes on them at the first light of day, before the dogs the birds or the rabbits have marred the beauty of the white landscape with their own marks of existence.

Though our farm was only a short four miles southeast of town, it was still very vulnerable to the consequences of Mother Nature's actions when she dumped and drifted snow all over the countryside. We had a very narrow gravel road that was our link to the outside world. The road was in the shape of an L, the longest leg running from Highway 83 to the bottom of the hill that marked the beginning of our farm's property. The road was laid out in such a manner that when a northwest wind came along with a winter delivery of snow, we had a high probability of becoming stranded by the snowdrifts that would form in the road.

Of course, to a kid, whether you grew up on a farm or in the city, any reason to not go to school is a good reason. I doubt that my sisters would agree, but I would bet that secretly even they enjoyed the consequences created by being snowed in by the winter weather.

The most memorable times of snowed-in isolation came when the winter storms were so large that the snowplows didn't come to rescue us from our peaceful isolation for anywhere from three to five days. Often these storms came along unpredicted; weathermen don't seem to be much better at forecasting now than they were back then. "Those weathermen don't know shit from shinola," my grandpa used to state. I didn't know what shinola was, but I understood that grandpa placed weathermen and newsmen in the same category.

While we did have a radio and a black-and-white TV, we lived far enough out in the boonies that the television antenna located on the roof of our farmhouse would receive and place mostly ghostly impressions on the television in our living room. We lived far enough out in the boonies that the radio would receive stations better at night than in the daytime, and those local stations that we did listen to in the daylight hours always went off the air at sunset.

When the family was snowed in, our main source of entertainment was provided by board games and playing cards. Cooking would even take on an added dimension, as experimenting with recipes that had never been previously tried seemed more feasible in light of the fact that you had nowhere to go; therefore, there was more time to experiment.

Meals on the farm were always eaten around the kitchen table with every member of the family in attendance. While there was never a time limit imposed on when a meal would end, this was even more true when marooned by the winter weather.

Meals generally started at the same times: breakfast at six a.m., lunch (dinner) at twelve noon, and supper at six p.m. The duration of each meal was dictated by the chores of the time of day. The evening meal generally lasted as long as any family business needed discussing, or until personal issues raised by any family member had been properly discussed, or until all the latest gossip and new jokes had been told. The evening meal would sometimes run into bedtime, which, of course, never came until after the dishes had been done by Mom and my sisters.

When we had really bad blizzards, the kitchen (and eating) would often take up the whole day from o'dark thirty in the morning, at the completion of morning chores, which still had to be done regardless of the weather. Mom would always make sure that breakfast was ready when Dad and I came back into the warm house after the morning chores were complete.

When snowed in, breakfast would often lead into a hot game of pitch or a long game of Monopoly, which would break up just in time for dinner (or lunch to those of you not sophisticated enough to understand the distinction between the two). This would then lead into an afternoon of gathering in the kitchen to watch it snow, watch Mom bake, and talk about things we didn't understand. These were discussions that generally led us to the conclusion that if we didn't understand it, it probably wasn't any of our business; therefore, we really didn't need to care or need to understand it.

Then it would be time for afternoon chores, which led to time for supper. And then, when supper was over, we would have time for another game of pitch or another board game, which led to getting the dishes done, and then going to bed.

Lying in your bed in the dark of night while a blizzard was raging outside provided a type of sleep that compared to those summer nights when your sleep was serenaded by a bass beat of thunder underscoring a symphony played by the endless harmony of rain. Winter's blizzard sleep is enhanced by the howling of a cold north wind, blowing so fierce that the trees shake, banging tree limbs against the side of the house. Knowing how cold it was outside as you snuggled up tight under layers of heavy blankets only amplified the chill factor of the wind, generating warmth that germinated dreams in Technicolor delight.

You dreaded having to get up in the morning or in the middle of the night to answer nature's call.

The sound of the snowplow finally making its way into the farmyard generated mixed feelings for each of us. It was a relief to know that we now had been reconnected to the outside world, yet at the same time, it was disconcerting to know that the Mother Nature–imposed family time was soon to be displaced by the reality of having to rejoin the rest of the world.

It seems that being snowed in provided our family with a time for the cleansing of our lives; a season for taking the time to lend an ear and listen to thoughts, troubles, and dreams and even to share tears that were not normally allowed because of the pressures that everyday life put on our time.

It was a time where the snow gave us an opportunity to cleanse our souls.

I doubt that we understood at the time just how lucky we really were.

CHAPTER SIX

THE SEASONS: SPRING

"I'll be go to hell."—Grandpa Farmer

Spring brought with it a renewal of the realization that all the adventures provided by farm life were accompanied by responsibilities that you would someday develop an appreciation for.

I certainly didn't hold any appreciation for those chores I was responsible for as a kid, but I somehow knew that I would later recall and develop an appreciation for the wisdom I had gained as each responsibility was dealt with.

There are times I seem to end up feeling sorry for the people I have met in my adult life that missed out on the opportunity of growing up on the farm. Farm kids were given specific chores to do throughout the year, most of which were required to be done daily, all of which proved to be useful in that process of learning how to use your head.

Chores that if not done properly, or in some cases just plain not done at all, had specific progressive disciplines that you were certain had been mandated by God. Disciplines that were enforced with a generous attitude that you didn't dare question; discipline policies that helped you to understand the importance of being a responsible member of the farm family.

The seasons of the year played a big part in the process of determining which of your chores you enjoyed the most. For example, the feeding of the chickens and the gathering of eggs each day was never a task that

I seemed to mind. Whether it was cold, hot, rainy, or sunny, it was a chore that was over quickly.

Watching the gate when Dad gave hay to the cows was no fun at all, especially in the dead of winter with the wind blowing hard from the north and the wind chill approaching sixty degrees below zero.

I think my favorite chore of the year was when we irrigated the corn and alfalfa fields, except for when my sisters did not follow through properly with their assigned chores. Apparently in the handbook for girl farm kids, the recommended discipline for general orneriness is to have them help their brother irrigate the corn and alfalfa fields.

Whenever my sisters were told to help me irrigate, I would plead with them to please stay in the pickup and listen to the radio while I did the irrigating.

The more they tried to help me, the more work they created for me to do. For example, repairing the damage they did to the soft banks of the earthen irrigation ditches that they would invariably end up walking on in their effort to stay out of the mud. Then tripping over and pulling out of the water the siphon tubes used to water the fields as they slapped wildly at the mosquitoes and flies that frequented the cornfields.

Irrigation season was long. It started in the spring and ended in the summer. Of course, if we had a lot of rain, irrigation season was easy. Rain meant calling the irrigation district and telling them to shut off the water, which led to more opportunities to fish and seek adventure with Yogi.

The spring season brought with it a newborn earth and helped you to understand the cycle of life, watching the countryside die each fall only to witness its resurrection in the spring.

For me it was in the spring months that I realized another year had passed by and that another year was starting. It was in the spring that I realized it was time to wake up from the slumber of winter and sharpen your mind so you could stay ahead of any kind of trouble that a new year would bring, trouble that was generated by the evil minds of sisters, or a dog anxious to explore the reawakened countryside in search of truth and adventure.

With spring came the work of preparing the fields for the new year's crops, the disking and the plowing, which led to the planting of the seeds. The sweet smell of the good soil on our farm being overturned by the plow in the brisk, spring morning air has yet to be duplicated by any candle or incense.

Spring brought with it the joy of watching the newborn calves playing in the fields, the sound of baby chicks in the hayloft. If you stopped and listened, you would hear a symphony of sound created by the world as it renewed itself for the adventures that a new year brings.

Spring also brought with it a reminder of the power that nature can unleash on all that live on this earth. Power unleashed in the form of floods and tornados, two natural events that reminded us that we are only stewards of the land we lived on.

I remember the spring that followed a winter when we had an unusual amount of snow. The drifts created by the wind and snow that year were so high that you could walk right up onto the roof of the house by simply walking up to the top of the drifts.

When the spring thaw came that year, it brought with it the floods that accompany too much water from too much snow added to the warm rains of springtime.

The rain and thawing snow created so much water that the ditches that ran adjacent to the gravel roads could not handle the volume. As the water had to go somewhere, it spilled out over the top of the roads and took the quickest route it could find to the river that was next to our farm.

One such route that the water followed was down the hill on the road that led to our farm. The water washed out onto the road and on down the hill, taking with it the earth that made up the road, leaving us with no way to get into town.

We ended up driving our family car over the cornfields between our farm and the neighboring farm to a place on top of the washed-out road where we could leave the car. For about a month the family would all pile into the pickup whenever we had to go to town or school, driving the pickup to the bottom of the washed-out hill, parking it beside the road, and hiking up to the top of the hill by walking in the pasture next to the road, then getting into the car we had parked on top of the hill and continuing our journey into town.

I remember when we discovered that the road was washed out, my grandpa uttered an expression that I am not sure I really understood, but one that I heard him use over and over again. "I'll be go to hell," he exclaimed.

The tornado season started in April and lasted into August. Tornados were one of those things you had to learn how to live with. They may come and they may not come, so it was best to know what to do in the event that one did show up.

We had a basement dug out underneath our house that was accessible through a door located in the floor of the kitchen inside the farmhouse, or you could enter through the storm cellar doors that were located outside on the west side of the house. We had drills so that we would know what to do if a tornado was ever spotted heading our way. These drills were held in both daylight and nighttime hours so that we would be ready no matter the time of day the tornado might come.

When a tornado did hit in an area that was close enough to drive to, the family would get in the car and take a drive to see the destruction caused by this force of nature. It was always a drive that would give you the proper respect for why we held the practice drills.

It seemed like every time we did have a storm that could harbor a tornado, the family would gather in the storm cellar, less my dad and my grandpa, as they would always stay upstairs looking out the windows to see if a tornado was really coming. I often wonder if they had seen one if they would have been able to get down the steps to the safety of the storm cellar before it would hit, or if they would have been sucked right out of the house and distributed into the fields, to be found later by the search teams.

In the spring we always had wind, lots of wind! I remember thinking that the wind was created by the fact that the earth was spinning around on its axis. Of course, it never occurred to me that on days the wind didn't blow, the earth was still spinning around that same axis.

The main thing about springtime was that the cold and gray of winter wouldn't have to be dealt with, at least for a while. It was warmer, and you could go outside without a coat on. Life was good!

Chapter Seven

The River

"Boy are you in trouble!"—Yogi

Less than a half a mile to the east of our family farm was a beautiful river. It's current was as strong as that of the Amazon River. At least that's how strong it seemed to a young farm kid. It was a river full of all the life you would expect for a river in the Midwestern part of this great country of ours.

One could encounter beaver, muskrat, deer, coyotes, jackrabbits, cotton-tail rabbits, and a wide variety of snakes and birds anytime you approached the river.

I had been warned of the dangers of the river in so many different voices, by so many different caring adults: "Don't you go near that river; you could drown," or, "If you go near that river you be careful; you could disappear and we would never see you again," and the fiercest of all prophesies, "If you go near that river you'll be grounded for the next ten years."

Of course, none of these warnings worked, as I was too young to understand the finality of drowning, and so full of wonder that the idea of disappearing sounded like a great adventure. The thought of being grounded held no terror in my mind, as being grounded meant that I was confined to the 180 acres of our farm.

Besides, I was under the influence of my faithful companion Yogi, who could convince me on a moment's notice that any day was a great day to go to the river.

I remember one warm summer day when I was about twelve years old; we had been forced to play indoors for a number of days due to some very heavy rain. The first day that broke with sunshine after those fierce storms was also without wind and seemed to be the perfect day for river adventure as far as Yogi was concerned. Yogi was a very persuasive dog and had me tagging along behind him headed for the river by nine o'clock on that beautiful day.

Of course, any time we found ourselves down by the river, we had to scout out all those areas that we had claimed as ours to see if anything had changed. We always had to see what Mother Nature or the local high school kids might have brought to our river.

The high school kids liked to go down to the river and do whatever it was that high school kids did. Sometimes they left things behind that would only enhance the adventure of the day.

This day, we discovered that Mother Nature had left us what appeared to be a bridge plank: a piece of wood some four inches thick, two feet wide, and eight feet in length. It was deposited into a large brush pile that was the creator of one of the best catfish holes on the river.

Yogi was so excited about this piece of wood that he immediately jumped into the river, swam out to the plank, and climbed on board. He then urged me to strip off my shoes and shirt so I could jump into the river, dislodge the plank from the brush pile that it had been snagged up in, and set it free. Once the plank was set free, its true potential for adventure became apparent.

As our newfound vessel began to match the speed of the river current, Yogi immediately assumed the head of our ship and summoned me to climb on board and straddle the bow. By the time I was able to climb onto the fast-drifting board, we had already drifted a few hundred feet downriver and this adventure was underway.

Yogi and I had both agreed that the river was our most favorite place for adventure; however, we were always restricted in our journeys by manmade barriers such as fences, or natural barricades like washouts and thickets. On this day, our newly provided water vessel had quickly extended the territorial rights of our river, and the swift river current was quickly taking us into uncharted, new territory.

In a short matter of time, we had already floated far past the island that was our landmark as the furthest, most southern point we had ever traveled down the river.

Too young to understand the potential consequences of a swift river current, and under the contagious influence of man's best friend, Yogi and I continued our journey headed for the Mississippi river. Well, at least we could have been headed for the Mississippi, as we had no idea how far it was we would end up going.

We quickly became fascinated by the wildlife that we were encountering: a large flock of geese in the still water that lay behind the far side of the island, and the beaver hut that sat just off the eastern bank of the river not a quarter of a mile from the island.

We discovered many natural springs feeding cold, fresh water into the warmer waters of the swift-flowing river, which required us to beach our new ship so we could investigate why the water was so cool on our legs when we drifted next to the dirt bank on the eastern banks of the river.

We encountered fish so large that we lifted our feet and paws out of the water for fear that they would bite off our toes.

Yogi got really good at maintaining his balance on this manmade log and was soon able to stand up and bark his approval at those things which seemed to cause dogs the need to bark. Then he would lay back down on the plank to stare into the water, and dip his ears, and nod that big head of his from side to side as he watched the fish swim by.

We soon noticed that as the shoreline and fish went swimming by, so did a good portion of the day. We did not have a watch to note time with, but it was obvious to us both that the sun was getting closer to the western horizon, and we decided it might be a good time to pull over, dock our newfound possession, and begin the walk back home.

Besides, we were both getting a little bit hungry!

It didn't take us long to realize that we might have a little problem. Once we got our wood plank out of the water, safely pulled free of the currents of the river, Yogi discovered that he was not able to smell anything that was close to anywhere we had ventured to before.

A quick scan of the countryside revealed a large steel bridge spanning the river not a quarter of a mile to our south, a bridge that I soon recognized as the one that my grandfather had driven us over on one of the many trips we took when we inspected the county roads, as was his duty as a county commissioner.

We climbed up on a bank that was a little higher than the rest of the land around the bridge and determined that this bridge was only a short distance from Highway 11. Highway 11 ran only two miles from our farm, but I also remembered that this bridge was far enough away from our farm that you generally had time enough to hear three or four songs on the radio before you got to it.

Using that God-given ability to relate time and distance to the speed that a car travels down the highway, and the fact that a normal song lasts a little more than three minutes, I was able to deduct that this bridge was about sixteen miles from our farm, as the crow flies.

Yogi looked at me as if to say, "Boy are you in trouble," as he put his head down and began walking in the direction of the highway—a highway that ended up taking us almost half an hour to get to.

As we walked I was reciting to Yogi a list of the possible consequences and accompanying progressive discipline we could be subjected to for the activities of this day, but he didn't seem interested as we continued our journey walking northwest along the shoulder of Highway 11.

Yogi may have had great vision, but I sometimes suspected that his ears didn't work right. "You know that you will never be able to see anything for what it really is unless you learn how to listen," I admonished my four-legged friend. I guess his ears did work a little, as his gate stopped abruptly and he cocked his head in my direction, making a grunting type noise that translated into something like, "You been listening to the Beatles again?"

"Actually," I began my reply to a dog that had already returned to the business of walking home, "I think I heard the thing about listening and seeing in Sunday school."

We hadn't walked an eighth of a mile along highway 11 when an old Ford pickup truck passed us and pulled over to the side of the road. It was driven by a farmer right out of the Norman Rockwell gallery, complete with straw hat, bib overalls, and chew firmly planted between cheek and gum, including the occasional drool that seems to ooze out the corner of the mouth belonging to the chewer of tobacco.

After some courteous conversation about who we were and the reason we were walking along the highway after five in the afternoon, our new friend shined the light of salvation on us when he told us that he knew exactly the location of our farm then indicated that he would be glad to take us home.

Without hesitation, Yogi showed that he had grasped an understanding of the situation as he quickly jumped into the back in of the farmer's truck then turning around and looking at me as if to say, "Hurry up and get in before he changes his mind," and we were off on the short, twenty-minute ride back to our farm.

When we turned off the highway onto the dirt road that led to our farm, our farmer savior of the day pulled his truck over along the road right at the bottom of the hill that led up to our farmhouse, got out of the pickup with that grin of knowledge that I noticed adults seemed to possess, and said, "I reckon you may want to get out here, then when you go walking up to the house, you can let your conscience guide you as to the story you tell your parents that will put an end to this journey."

He opened up the tailgate of his pickup so that Yogi and I could get out, let fly with a well-compacted spit of chew, touched the brim of his hat, and said, "You boys behave now." He then slid into the driver's side of the old Ford, turned it around, and headed off in a cloud of dust.

Yogi sat on the side of the road as if to say, "You go on ahead up the hill. I will be right behind you."

The end of this journey produced a couple of parents that didn't even realize we had been gone. It seems that their activities that day had led them on their own adventures, which kept them in town up until just before we came walking up the hill to the farmyard.

In the days that followed, whenever I shared the adventures of this day with my friends, they would just give me a look of disgust and disbelief, doubting that we could ever end up so far from home aboard a piece of wood.

So Yogi and I decided to keep this adventure to ourselves, and just to show that we had good common sense, we imposed our own one month's worth of confinement to the 180-plus acres of our farm. It seemed like the right thing to do.

Yogi did not seem to be too distraught, as he laid down beside me for some well-deserved rest. I still remember that particular day spent on the river with Yogi and wonder just who that farmer was that gave us a lift home from the river.

CHAPTER EIGHT

WATCHING THE NEWS WITH GRANDDAD

*"Remember, your mind is like a parachute: it will work
only as long as it is open."—Grandpa Farmer*

Sir Walter Raleigh, who he was is still a mystery, what he smelled like was well known, at least in the house in town on 5th street, where grandpa's pipe was allowed to broadcast his scent.

Out on the farm, my other granddad was partial to a good cigar.

I remember sitting with each of my grandfathers, listening to the news on the radio, or watching the news on television. Each grandfather liked to smoke as they relaxed, and watching the news was for them a form of relaxation.

I can still see the chaos created in the air by smoke as it swirled into action when they would blow it into the living room air. The sunlight streaming in the windows showing off the smokes dance of indifference as it sought to fill every gap in the room that it could find.

Smoke floating from the bowl of the pipe, or off the end of the cigar, revolving as in a spiral staircase, around and around rising higher and higher as it sought to escape the confines of the house.

Laying on the living room floor, studying my granddad as he relaxed with pipe or cigar, I was transformed to the damp earthen floor deep in the woods of the northern back country, a lake just ahead, steam rising from its waters, the lake busily feeding its attributes with the things that this earth required of them to be deemed streams.

My Granddads were twin lakes, giving their young stream whatever he needed to gain strength. They continually provided me with gentle waves of knowledge. When like a flooded rushing stream I would begin to grow out of control, they could control that flow of thoughts I was thinking, until once again they could see that balance was restored.

One grandfather was a pharmacist. He lived in town in a large house which had in it one of those octagon-shaped color televisions.

The awards on the wall of his home said that he was highly esteemed by his colleagues and peers. The phone calls from those needing care, said he was more trusted than those doctors they choose not to call.

The other grandfather was a farmer. He lived in a trailer house just to the south of our farmhouse, which had in it an older black-and-white television.

The features of his face showed the years of sweat and toil working on his farm, the calloused hands told of his perseverance.

Their integrity was never challenged.

They each took their roles as a grandpa very seriously. They each could sense when confusion was taking over. They knew exactly when to intervene. Their wisdom was always perfectly revealed. Their follow up was never forgotten.

It seemed that my parents always knew when one of my Granddads had taught me a lesson. Each grandfather understood just how important it was to keep mom and dad informed of what they were teaching, always honoring the sovereignty of parents.

In town Grandpa Pharmacist had cable TV. Out in the country Grandpa Farmer had a shaky old antenna that worked best if a storm was coming.

I remember that most of what you saw on Grandpa Farmer's television looked more like news given by ghosts. Only when a storm was imminent could you recognize the newsmen that were telling you the news of the day. Radio was clearly the best way to get the news when out on the farm.

Grandpa Pharmacist could easily get his grandkids to come into town to watch TV. I remember that some Sunday nights we would go into town to watch *Bonanza* and *Walt Disney's Wonderful World of Color.*

But when it came to the news, it didn't really matter much which television you were watching. It also didn't much matter which grandpa you where watching the news with. Each one had his own method of talking back to the television about the news that was being broadcast.

Grandpa Pharmacist would smoke his pipe and chuckle as each news item was read.

Grandpa Farmer, with his cigar resting in an ashtray, would often be grazing through the newspaper while the news was on, admonishing everyone in the room, "You're watching a bunch of damn fools. It's all a bunch of foolishness. If you believe those fools on TV, you're just as foolish as they are."

Grandpa Farmer was one that didn't really believe we landed a man on the moon. He used to tell me that it was all staged in movie studios in California. He claimed that most things of foolishness came from California. I only knew that Disneyland was in California, and it looked pretty cool to me!

Each grandfather taught me to be very careful as to what you believed when watching the news on television or listening to it on the radio. They both enjoyed the farm and market reports, and often would show more emotion during those broadcasts, usually in the form of disgust lamenting at the prices of corn and fat cattle.

With the news, they each had a proper portion of distrust in the content of those stories being read over the airwaves.

It wasn't until years later that I understood just how wise these two old men were.

Grandpa Farmer used to tell me, "Boy," he called me boy for as long as I could recall. "Boy," he would say, "remember, your mind is like a parachute: it will work only as long as it is open."

Each grandfather taught me to be careful about those things that I heard, and to believe only those things that I could fully understand.

I think it was my grandpas that got me to thinking about what things it was that I was going to pursue in my life. I remember having discussions with both of them about the things that make you happy, the things that confuse your thoughts, and even those things that made you mad.

I don't remember which of them might have said it. Maybe neither of them actually said it like I understand it now, but I know that everyone ends up doing something. Most people end up doing things that they really never wanted to do, but they had to provide for a family, or maybe they felt obliged to carry on a business that their family had run.

But some folks learn what things in this world make their hearts beat faster, they find out what things really interest them, what things give them real joy. Those are the people that are the lucky ones. My granddads used to tell me, "Find out what it is that makes you happy, listen to your heart, and let it tell you what things you really have a passion for, then pursue those things. Hang on to them, never let them go, and you'll be alright!"

Those two great lakes of Grandpa never rose up into a storm, were never covered with raging waves, even when the harshness of life tried to stir them up. They were always a tranquil harbor, whether seeking shelter from confusion, or seeking a cove from injustice their calm resolve was always ready to settle the storm.

Words of encouragement flowed from the mouths of Lake Grandpa, regulated with temperance like a cool salve on a burning itch.

They were never ones that would put you in over your head. Their knowledge of your abilities was always greater than the reality of your fears.

It took me years to figure these things out. Only after I finally admitted that I couldn't do everything on my own, and I had been filled with the Holy Spirit of God, was I was able to truly understand the sage wisdom of these two great men. And I have missed them more every day since.

Chapter Nine
Grandma's Advice

"Well, I'll be jiggered."—Grandma

There are natural laws of physics with which no wise person will argue. There are equally true laws that govern the lives of all children with regard to the words that flow out of the mouths of our grandmothers. One such law that required the highest level of attention from all children is, "When your grandmother speaks, you had better pay attention."

I had the good fortune of being able to spend time with both sets of my grandparents.

My family lived in a farmhouse that was less than fifteen yards from the trailer house that was home to my dad's parents.

My mom's parents lived in town, which was about four miles from our farm.

Each of my grandmothers had a strong faith in God, and what appeared to be an equally strong belief that children are to be seen and not heard. They believed this especially in any situation when other adults were around. But if it was just grandma and you, you would be hard-pressed to find a better friend.

My dad's mom was a big baseball fan. During baseball season I had a daily routine that included a visit with Grandma Baseball after my grandpa had gone down and picked up the mail from our mailbox. You see, living in the country, the daily newspaper was delivered by a rural mail carrier.

Grandma Baseball had a special place in her heart for the Chicago Cubs. Later on in life I discovered that this affection for the Cubs was really a form of disease. Some even told me that it was a special type of mental illness. To others it was considered an addiction that could be treated by any of a number of different twelve-step programs.

Grandma Baseball's knowledge of the history of baseball was unsurpassed by any other member of my family, a fact that was not well known in our family, as she was also very quiet.

Even when compared to the baseball knowledge of Grandpa Pharmacist, who would venture to Arizona each February and take in the entire spring training season, Grandma Baseball's knowledge of lifetime batting averages and pitchers' records could not be disputed.

By the time I finally made it over to Grandma's trailer to memorize the daily sports section, she had already read it and updated her own vast memory. She held my attention with many discussions about the greats of the game. I learned more from her than I ever learned from those know-it-alls that did the game of the week on TV.

I would have given anything to throw a baseball like Bob Gibson or hit a ball as far as Harmon Killebrew. I remember spending many hours throwing a baseball as hard as I could up against the west side of our barn, playing out in my own imagination the ninth inning of many imaginary World Series seventh games.

Years later when witnessing my very first major league baseball game in New York at Yankee Stadium, it was Grandma Baseball that I thought about as I sat watching the game, not three rows up from the field on the third base side of the diamond.

When at the other grandmother's house in town, baseball was not the order of discussion, for my grandmother in town had little interest in sports; she was more a spectator of people.

She knew every single person in the county, or so it seemed. Knew how big their families were, where they lived, what their family income was, the grades they received in high school, what they bought and didn't buy at the store, when they were born, and when they were going to die. Well, it seemed like she knew when they were going to die.

She had a way of expressing herself that was unique, and her favorite expression was, "Well, I'll be jiggered." I never understood what it was to be jiggered, but if Grandma said she was, I'm sure that it was true.

I wasn't too sure about what a psychologist was, but I thought she would have been a good one. Grandma Psychologist also knew what I was thinking before I even thought it. It was a mystery to me then, and it still mystifies me to this day how she not only could predict what I was going to do but also how she correctly predicted those things I would do long after she had gone to glory.

Grandma Psychologist knew that I needed constant watching and discipline. She knew when to discipline and when to reward. And though it seemed I always got more discipline than reward, she always knew that exact moment when I needed a special reward. Like after having finished mowing the grass that surrounded her house on Fifth Street, she would present a special reward that generally came in the form of an ice-cold bottle of cola. We did not get much cola on the farm, as it was a luxury that our family farm's budget could not often afford.

I can still remember to this day the feeling of joy that I experienced at the prospect of getting to drink an entire ice-cold glass bottle of cola all by myself.

I can still close my eyes and remember the exact taste of it today!

Sometimes my sisters and I would all end up in town together at Grandma's. We would occasionally have to split the ice-cold bottle of cola. Oh the amount of time it took for that bottle of cola to be split! You see, it had to be split up into three equal shares. Most times it took us longer to decide who would be tasked with the splitting up of the cola than it actually took to perform the task.

You see, the person that did the dividing got last picks. Oh the precision used to ensure that equal portions were present in each of the three glasses!

I remember that watching her grandkids enjoy an ice-cold cola seemed to have the effect of loosening up Grandma Psychologist, which would allow her to share her sense of humor. The type of humor that says a burp is funny. When Grandma Psychologist would join us in an ice-cold cola, she would generally finish her bottle with a lengthy and loud belch. "BBbbwwwweeeeeerrrpppp, watch out, I'm goin' to blow up," she would proclaim at the end of each outburst.

Grandma Psychologist had a particular place in the dining room that she used to stand in and watch what was going on in the world outside. She would provide a commentary about the activities that she was witnessing as my sisters and I would be enjoying our ice-cold colas. I can see her now, at her station in the dining room, next to the windows, looking out the front of the house, providing a colorful play-by-play of the sometimes strange happenings that made up the day to day living in our small Midwestern community.

Grandma had her own colorful description for most of the characters in our town.

She particularly enjoyed watching the neighbors that lived across the street to the north whenever they took a notion to load their pet Shetland pony into their 1966 Mustang automobile to take it for a ride. "Land O' Goshen," she would declare. "There goes that crazy lady taking her fool horse for another ride in the country. I wonder how they ever got that horse to get into and out of that car."

It was quite the sight, but one that was more common in this rural town that seemed to be full of what would be uncommon sights in most other towns.

I fondly remember those days spent with my grandmothers. Each day was special in its own way, depending on which grandma I had the privilege to be with. Each grandmother was willing to share her own special type of love and wisdom, wisdom that I am convinced God was whispering in their ears—a divine directive that they knew full well the importance of me hearing.

Lessons taught with love that come floating back into my memories when watching a baseball game, smelling a freshly mowed yard, or tasting an ice-cold cola.

CHAPTER TEN
COWS

"You need a bucket with a wickerbill on it."—Uncle Rancher

We never had a lot of cows on our farm. I think we had somewhere around thirty cows on the farm year-round. Of course, to a kid, thirty cows is a lot.

Every year it seemed that one of our cows would give birth to twin calves, much to the disgust of my dad. I didn't understand why Dad was not happy about this event. It seemed to me that he should have been pleased. I mean if one cow on a small farm has two calves that would increase the value of the farm, right?

What I learned was that the mother cow would usually choose one of the two baby calves, usually the biggest one, and nurse and raise that one while leaving the other calf to fend for its own life. Usually the abandoned calf would not survive.

The handbook of rules for the farm must state that the age of accountability for the taking care of baby calves is ten years of age, as one spring day in my tenth year I was assigned the duty of being the mother to any twin calf that was rejected by its mother.

The great potential of this new responsibility escaped me at the moment, as I was not fully impressed that I had been given the responsibility to care for animals that were larger than a chicken.

Being a ten-year-old I was unaccustomed to the art of deal making. Not that it really mattered, as I think my dad probably had the power of veto over any suggestions that I may have wanted to make. This deal seemed to be pretty sweet for a ten-year-old kid. This deal gave me full ownership of all the animals that, as their substitute mother, I could keep alive.

It was a deal that my uncle must have thought made a lot of sense, as he quickly came on board to the concept and added his herd to my list of potential clients.

The wisdom possessed by a ten-year-old does not normally include that which is needed to teach a baby calf how to suck milk from first a bottle, and then from a bucket conveniently equipped with a nipple. Or of the subsequent knowledge needed to then understand the task of knowing what a baby calf needs to eat in order to become a healthy yearling.

The potential of this whole deal was mind-boggling. I was overwhelmed by my good fortune. How could my wise father be so blind as to see that I would soon have more cows then he had? I would soon compete with the largest herds in the county, maybe even end up with a ranch that equaled that of that Cartwright family on television.

I soon began to learn of all those trappings that come with the ownership of cattle. This ten-year-old found out quickly that the capital required to raise livestock was indeed substantial.

In my role of raising chickens from baby chicks to full-grown laying hens, I was allowed to keep a portion of the money earned from selling eggs to the butter factory in town. Of course, I needed some of that money to pay for the supplies needed in raising chickens.

My parents helped a lot by providing me with some great birthday gifts on my ninth and tenth birthdays. A complete set of twenty-four nests made from galvanized steel one year, and the following year a new grain feeder and chicken water tank complete with a heater to keep the water from freezing in the winter.

But the money required to raise a baby calf from a baby to a full-grown cow was beyond my comprehension. The equipment that I would need and where to get it was described to me by my uncle. He told me I would need a bucket with a wickerbill attached to it. A wickerbill could have been just about anything in my uncle's mind. In this case a wickerbill was a nipple.

My share of the profits from the eggs sold in town at the local butter factory (eggs sold for anywhere from nineteen cents to twenty-five cents a dozen) soon provided me with what I needed to pay back my dad for the bucket with the long nipple on it, and for the nipple that fit perfectly on the old soda pop bottle that I chose to use in teaching the calves how to suck.

My uncle fronted me the money for the first bag of milk replacement formula, which we purchased at the local feed store in town. All I had left to do was to teach that first calf how to suck from a bottle and I was on my way to fame and riches.

My dog, Yogi, proved to be a very valuable business partner in this endeavor, as it was his interest that provided me with the breakthrough I needed to get the first calf sucking from the bottle. After hours of being unable to convince my newly formed herd that the ability to suck was essential to the ability for it to survive, it was Yogi that stood up on his hind legs and started licking the milk formula from the outside of the bottle around the bottom edge of where the nipple attached to the bottle.

This provided me with the brilliant idea of simply pouring some of the formula straight down the throat of that calf, which led to the calf being able to understand that this was good stuff and that it felt good inside the calf's belly. The sucking was soon so prevalent that I was able to graduate my student calf from a bottle to a bucket within a matter of days.

I guess my dad did not think that I would be as successful as I was at teaching a baby calf how to suck. Over the next few years I didn't lose any of the calves given to me by my dad or my uncle.

By the time I was sixteen I had a herd of six cows, and had fattened up and shipped off to market enough fattened beef that I was able to purchase my own car when I was a senior in high school.

Over the years, those baby calves had to compete with my dog, Yogi, for my attention and affection. Of course, these calves did not possess the personality or the persuasive powers for adventure of that wonder dog Yogi .

Whenever I would come out of the house, those baby calves would come running. Of course, they identified me as their primary source of food and were only intent on trying to coerce another bucket of formula out of me. I guess to a baby calf, it seemed that anytime was a good time to eat. I understood this concept, as this was very similar to the thoughts about eating of a kid growing up on the farm.

I was a blessed child; favor had been given to me in ways I did not at the time understand. It may not have been the cattle of a thousand hills, but it seemed to be a pretty good start.

Chapter Eleven
Raising Pigs

"Pigs are cleaner than people."—Schoolteacher

I suspect that pigs are demon possessed. I suspect this as pigs are the one animal that generated the greatest fears in my mind while growing older and wiser on the farm.

Fear is something that we all must learn how to conquer. I would venture that those things that stir up fear in a farm boy are greatly different from those things that increase the heart rate of a city kid. My own lessons in the handling of fear began innocently enough with adventures that always seemed to involve pigs.

It seems that I have read many articles stating that pigs are among the smartest of those animals you will find on a farm. I wonder what illegal drug the authors that wrote those articles had mixed in with their Cheerios.

While we didn't have the privilege of raising sheep on our farm, I did have the misfortune of encountering them as a teenager when working on the ranch that my uncle ran. This is important in order to give pigs some credit.

I was given the task of trying to herd some sheep that had gone astray into a pen that had on it a gate that had to be at least twenty feet wide. It could have been fifty feet wide; it would not have made any difference to these blind woolies. I doubt that a sheep has within its genetic code the intelligence needed to understand what an open gate is.

Sheep, it seems, have some type of genetic code that provides an instinct in which they must crash through any fence that stands between them and the Promised Land that the herder is trying to put them into.

I doubt that the eyes of a sheep can even begin to process the light captured in the lens of their eyes that has been reflected by an open gate.

It seems there is an instinct that blocks the frontal lobes of the sheep brain from being able to process the data that would instruct the legs of the sheep to walk calmly into a pen through an open gate.

I would agree that only when compared to sheep do pigs indeed exhibit a higher level of intelligence. When compared to the height of a rut in the middle of a previously muddy country road, the intelligence of a pig would never measure as high as the deepest rut.

The intellect level of the average pig could not possibly stretch as high as the average height of an ant!

Yogi and I held many debates about which animals are the smartest. Of course, dogs being as intelligent as humans was a given, so they were not included in this discussion. Yogi was more impressed with an animal's bravery than their brains. He had a great deal of respect for the badger and liked to remind me of the battle he had with one outside the chicken coop one night, a battle that got longer each time he brought it up.

"Pigs are cleaner than people" was something that I had heard my schoolteacher say once. Of course, this makes no sense to anyone, as we all know that pigs like laying around in the mud and slop that is contained within a pig lot. Of course this only served to convince me further that I was right in my assessment of teachers and the amount of knowledge that they really possessed.

I also remember hearing someone once say that "animals were created to remind men to take a bath," which made about as much sense as eating beets, or taking a bath more than once a week, but never mind all this analysis. Since we did not raise sheep, pigs were undeniably the dumbest of animals that graced our little family farm.

Getting back to that first time I learned how to do battle with my own fears: I first confronted real fear one cold, windy night in November while on a mission that required me to make my way through the dark of a moonless night some one hundred yards from the farmhouse out to the hog shed.

This particular moonless night had been made darker by events of that day, which included the assassination of a U.S. president. The environment of a moonless night, the events of the day, and the overactive mind of a ten-year-old formed the thoughts that led me to think that the unknown presidential assassin was surely lying in wait for me, as he must have known that I had to routinely go out and check on the baby pigs in the hog shed each night before I went to bed at ten o'clock.

Oh, I forgot to mention the rats, a fear for which would only pour gasoline on the fire of fear that was already ignited in my mind as they went scurrying in every direction, including the direction that was directly toward me, the minute I opened the door to the dark hog shed.

And on this night, fate added a little extra as I was greeted at the door to the hog shed not only by rats but also by a squeal that can only come from a baby pig that had been sat on by the much larger mama pig. The dark, the rats, the squeal, the assassins waiting to ambush me from the trees, all gave me goose bumps the size of warts up and down my arms and legs.

I was able to defeat my fear and continue into the dark of the hog shed, as I knew that I had to investigate the squeal. As I approached the particular pen that was the source of the horrifying sound, I climbed up on the lower board of the pen so that I could peer over the top board of the pen and see what the heat lamp inside would reveal. What I saw was an introduction into just how gruesome and cruel the farm can be, a sight so hideous that it is left better untold, so hideous that it increased the level of fear I was feeling up to and beyond the point that trauma must begin.

The sight of a large, hungry sow that had turned carnivorous toward her young, fueled by fear and trauma I had never experienced before, created a frenzy of spontaneous behavior that had I been able to duplicate and recreate could have turned me into a world-class athlete.

It was a spontaneous reaction that fueled the world-record speed with which I raced my way back to the safety of the farmhouse from that pig pen of hell. I doubt that my feet touched the ground more than eight or nine times on the way back to our house.

Thank goodness my mom knew how to deal with fear and trauma. While my dad was telling me to calm down and quit making mountains out of molehills, my loving mom was preparing a hot cup of cocoa complete with marshmallows, knowing that with this elixir, along with her love, my trauma and fears would be defeated.

My father had a great bedside manner for dealing with those same sows when it came time to send them to market. It seems that the female pig has some type of genetic self-survival code implanted into that big head of hers that provides them with an inability to walk up the loading chute that leads to the back of the truck that would end up delivering said pigs to their final and just reward at the butcher market.

That same weapon (a two-by-four made from treated Douglas fir) my father would use to send our farm's meanest barnyard rooster to the boiling pot was also the persuader that would invariably coax these barnyard behemoths into the back of the stock truck.

The squeals of protest that those mad sows made would only be drowned out by my dad's voice uttering words that I would never use for fear of spending the rest of my life with a bar of soap stuck in my mouth.

My fear of pigs was further fueled by the endless stories that you seemed to always hear on the radio newscast about people being trampled to the ground and then eaten by mad sows somewhere on a farm, somewhere in the Midwest.

Over the years, I was able to defeat my fear of pigs. In fact, I had been so able to defeat my fears that by the time I approached my teen years I was able to prove my bravery around swine to anyone that wanted to watch, spending an entire afternoon doing nothing but chasing pigs (young or old—it didn't matter) around the pen just west of our hog house.

In fact, I became so good at this that tales of my abilities began to spread into town via those relatives who had witnessed me and my adeptness at chasing pigs.

When the city kids would come out to watch me exhibit my abilities, they were soon misled by my craftiness and great skill into believing that this was a type of fun they could also enjoy.

Then Yogi joined in the fun and convinced them to come on into the pen and join the fun, as he too would join in the activities, chasing and nipping at the tails and hoofs of those innocent swine.

Of course, Yogi and I would quickly exit the pig yard once the unsuspecting city kids got close to that point in time when the pigs started getting annoyed. Yogi and I would then sit back and take great pleasure in watching those unsuspecting city kids turned into sniveling cowards by some of the biggest sows on our farm.

Of course, once our quota for entertainment was satisfied, I would take even greater pleasure in proving my bravery by jumping into the pen and showing those sows who the boss really was by chasing them until the foam started frothing from their mouths, earning high praise from the appreciative city kid for saving their lives from those vicious sows.

Every now and then I sometimes catch myself drifting away in thought towards a misguided dream of someday returning to and owning a little farm complete with all those animals that made my growing up such an adventure; all of those animals except, of course, for pigs.

Chapter Twelve
Raising Chickens

"You kids stop that! You'll bruise the meat. Hold onto that chicken and bring it over here."—Grandma Baseball

I don't remember how it became my responsibility. I can only assume that it was decided one day as the Holy Trinity sat around the breakfast table. "I say we make the boy responsible for the care of all operations related to chickens on the family farm," said our Creator. "To feed and water them daily, to collect the eggs each afternoon after school lets out. To each evening ensure that the entire population of chickens is safely accounted for in the chicken shed, and that the doors are securely fastened in order to keep the varmints from feasting on them while they sleep."

And with this edict, the work of creation was completed!

Not that I minded the task. I mean I had to get out of bed every day anyway. And the chicken coop wasn't that far away. And chickens can be pretty entertaining to a kid.

It was a task that I gladly accepted, but it wasn't without its challenges, the main one being that of keeping Yogi from killing the chickens and eating all the eggs. He didn't really mean them any harm, the chickens that is. He just liked chasing them!

The eggs, he thought they were delicious.

Every year around the first part of June, our farm was the host for a weekend event meant to fill the freezers with enough dressed-out chickens to meet the demand of the entire family for the rest of the year.

You have heard the old saying, "There is more than one way to kill a chicken"? I doubt that my dad or grandpa had any use for this logic, as it seemed they knew of only one way to start the process of harvesting chickens. That was by lopping off the poor chicken's head with an ax.

This act of beheading our farm's poultry was reserved expressly for the elder men of the farm. Dad and Grandpa went about this task with great professionalism; it was as if they had been commissioned for this work by going through some sort of an ordination processes. They went to great lengths in sharpening the ax they used, to the point that I'm sure it could split the fine hair of a frog.

The task of sorting out those chickens chosen for the honor of laying eggs from those chosen for the family freezer was carefully directed by Dad and Grandpa. The sorting out process was so smooth and efficient that I was certain that they had planned it out after watching NASA launch manned spacecraft. They would meticulously create a flow that would not back up the process of scalding, plucking, cutting, and wrapping that was being carried out by the women in the yard next to the house.

My task was that of catching the unsuspecting chicken and handing it over to the elders for the beheading. To do this I had invented a tool that I should have patented. It was a six-foot length of number nine wire with a hook curled into one end, which I would use to snag a leg on those chickens chosen for the sacrifice.

The funny thing about the reactions of a chicken that has just had its head severed from its body is that the chicken doesn't seem to understand that its life has been ended by that ax. We kids took great delight at letting a chosen few chickens suddenly get away from us after this dreadful but necessary deed had been accomplished for the entertainment of watching the headless chicken bounce around the barnyard.

Of course, one of the grandmothers would always end this fun by admonishing us, "You kids stop that! You'll bruise the meat. Hold onto that chicken and bring it over here."

Of course, this annual ritual led to the need for another annual ritual: the ritual that required my dad to place an order at the local hatchery in town each January for replacement chickens.

The replacement chickens would arrive each year around Easter, which I think was just coincidental. The arrival of anywhere from one hundred to two hundred baby chickens expanded my duties considerably.

I mentioned that Yogi liked to chase adult chickens. Let me mention now that baby chickens had the ability to completely change the behavior of my astute partner in adventure.

I never understood if it was the high-pitched peeping or just the flurry of motion with which baby chickens did everything they did that would get Yogi all excited, but keeping him away from those new baby chicks was a full-time job.

For not only the protection of the baby chicks but also to ensure that Yogi would not turn into a mass killer, we created a chicken nursery in the hayloft of our family barn. The loft was transformed into a chicken nursery by the creative use of chicken wire, a couple of bales of hay, three or four feed troughs, and one of the finest homemade brooders you ever saw. You know, one of those things that have heat lamps in them so that the baby chickens don't get cold.

I was always afraid that the preciously cute baby chickens would spontaneously ignite, transforming into premature barbeque in the middle of the night by getting too close to those heat lamps that we borrowed from the hog shed.

But the brooders seemed to always do the job. Yogi was always kept at bay, except for a mishap that will forever remain in the annals of untold farm stories. Each year when the chicks reached the age of a teenage chicken, we would open the door to the barn allowing the hundreds of teenage chickens the freedom to make their way down to the farmyard.

Of course, these poor innocent, formerly baby chickens had no idea what the farmyard was all about. Their confusion was obvious as we ushered the chaotic mass of feathers towards the chicken coop, where they would take up residence with those chickens that had survived the annual chicken slaughter.

Now, in order to survive the annual chicken slaughter, you had to be one of the top layers of eggs on the farm or the biggest and meanest rooster in the barnyard.

It was easy enough to identify those hens that laid the most eggs; they only numbered about thirty, and each had some type of an interesting identifying mark. To a farm kid, animal identification becomes very easy: you get to know all the animals on the farm pretty well after you spend so much time with them each day.

It was really easy to identify the meanest rooster, as there was only one mean roster, and he was pretty hard to ignore.

The rooster that ruled over our barnyard was by my grandpa's account at least fifty years old. Grandpa claimed that this particular roster was already on the farm when he bought it in 1914.

This roster stood a good twenty-four inches tall and had a spur on the back of each of his legs that curled up into a weapon that gave you bone-chilling goose bumps just by looking at it.

This king of the barnyard was not afraid of anything or anyone that turned his back to him, and he could run at least thirty miles per hour for the distance of fifty yards.

I once saw him go after one of our big old mean Hereford bulls. He sent that bull running right through the board fence that was in place around the water tank just northwest of the barn.

I was always very thankful that it was over sixty yards from the chicken house to the front gate of our yard. And even more thankful to our Creator in heaven that I was able to run one mile per hour faster than Mr. King of the Barnyard.

I will never forget that brisk fall day when Mr. King of the Barnyard met his maker. The day he made the mistake of challenging my dad, who just happened to be standing next to a six-foot-long two-by-four, which that wily old rooster obviously had overlooked.

That particular day, my dad and I were busy building a new wagon that we would use in hauling corn from the field to the barn. Somewhere in the excitement of wagon construction my dad offended Mr. King of the

Barnyard by turning his back on the old crow. This was deemed as an insult to the old cock, requiring that he defend his honor by taking on my dad, thus reestablishing his domain and rightful position of King of the Barnyard.

My dad was not what you would call a good multitasker. His work ethic gave rise to a desire that was intent on finishing the project at hand, which in this case was the new wagon.

Mr. Wily Old Rooster was showing his age by exhibiting a need for some corrective vision in his eyesight, as he was less than two feet away from my dad before he realized he had overlooked the two-by-four.

He was about a foot from my dad when he probably began to feel the leading edge of the wind created by the push of air out in front of the powerful swing of that two-by-four as it came sweeping down to a point of first contact with poor Mr. Rooster, right below the red comb that sat upon his proud and soon to be misguided head.

The sound that was created by the contact of that six-foot two-by-four in launching that rooster's head four rows deep into the cornfield directly west of the barn must have been similar to the sound of a baseball headed for the Green Monster at Fenway Park off the wooden bat of Babe Ruth.

When the dust settled from this unprovoked assault by my dad, there was an eerie moment of never-heard-before barnyard silence. Time seemed to stop, and every chicken in the barnyard gazed upon that headless pile of feathers that was once the King of the Barnyard.

I can only imagine that the joy I felt welling up in my heart, created by a realization that I would no longer need to anticipate the unknown location of this barnyard bully as I innocently strolled from place to place on the farm, was shared by every old hen in the barnyard that had experienced the loving weight of that old rooster as he performed his duties over the years.

For myself, and all the chickens in the yard, we had been liberated from an existence of having to race for survival from this menace.

That night we had a fine meal of boiled rooster, appropriately followed by apple pie à la mode and rooster stories that carried late into the night.

Chapter Thirteen
Country School

"Since it was a one-room school, you had the added benefit of being able to re-educate yourself each year with the basic fundamentals, as they were taught in grades kindergarten through eight."—Benefits of the Country School

The District 14 Schoolhouse was located about two miles from our family farm, just close enough that you had options as to the method of going to school, the most boring of which was being driven in one of the family vehicles. You also had the option of taking what could be a thrilling bike ride on the gravel-laden roads, subjecting your legs to the nipping of crazed dogs at each farm that you passed, or a routinely boring journey by foot if you chose to walk down those same roads used by the cars. The last option was one of adding unknown excitement by detouring from those roads and taking whatever path you chose while traversing the multiple miles over the hill and dale of our neighbors' farms.

The latter journey was made more exciting by the potential of running into one of our neighbors' bulls that may just happen to be grazing on the same section of land that you had chosen to walk on. Or by an encounter with the unknown power of electricity that some farmers chose to run through certain wires in the fences you had to go over, under, or through.

My sisters rarely approved of this adventurous route when we made the journey to school together. I guess it was their lack of the required amount of foot speed needed to outrun one ton of bull, or the lack of coordination needed to hurdle a five-foot-high barbed-wire fence without breaking stride in the act of avoiding hand-to-hoof combat with the angry bovine.

Or perhaps it was the lack of understanding about the powers of the electricity that was contained within the wires of those electric fences. You never knew which wire the farmers would put electricity in. We didn't know enough about electricity at the time to understand what an insulator was, which would have given us the knowledge needed to determine which wire was electrified. All we knew was that if you grabbed the wrong wire, it was going to hurt.

For me, electric fences created a need for understanding that would lead me into entirely new worlds of adventure as I grew older. But for now, all we wanted to do was get to school.

The schoolhouse was also far enough away from our farm that when you were not there, it was the last place you would think about.

The building was built of brick in the early 1900s and consisted of a single room with a basement, which was just enough space in which to begin learning those fundamentals adults said we needed to survive life in the world in which they had put us.

Since it was a one-room school, you had the added benefit of being able to re-educate yourself each year with the basic fundamentals, as they are taught in grades kindergarten through eight.

The number of students varied from year to year, depending on whether the family farms in the area were making enough money. However, I do not recall that we ever had more than seventeen or eighteen total students at one time in the wonderful years I had the privilege to attend this hollowed ground of learning.

We moved to the farm when I was in the third grade. Worse, we moved to our farm from a small town—key word, "town"; thus, I was a city boy in the eyes of those male students already enrolled at District 14.

You see, to a farm boy, there are few things in life worse than having to hang out with a kid that was not raised on, and still living on, the farm. Those differences reported in the beliefs of Republicans and Democrats or Catholics and Protestants are much easier to understand when compared to understanding the thought processes used by a farm boy in his evaluation of a kid that grew up in the city. Remember that to a farm kid, a city constituted any place that was not a farm.

Loyalty was the first ideal that farm kids looked for in anyone wishing to join their select ranks. My new classmates wanted to instill in me the kind of loyalty that would conclusively prove to them that I had what it took to be one of them: basically a loyalty that can only come from a heart that has no fear of the teacher.

There was an unwritten process, not so unlike that used in the initiation of fraternity or sorority members at higher education institutions, which was used to prove that you had the mettle to become a real country school student. It was a process that was virtually impossible to understand until you became one of the older kids in the school, which required being promoted into the seventh and eighth grades. I guess the thing that made it impossible to understand was that this process was made up as you went along.

Up until we moved to the farm and I began my career as a country school student, I had always considered myself to be a good kid. Before we moved to the farm I had an opportunity to prove this to my sisters one day when I was in the second grade. You see, there was a girl that was always picking on me. Her name escapes me, but I think it was something like Jezebel.

One day when school got out, Jezebel decided that it was time for a showdown. Waiting for me to walk across the school playground that I had to cross in order to get home, she pounced on me when I was in between the slides, the teeter-totters, and the swing sets.

I immediately took the offensive and found myself sitting on her chest, ready to beat her into submission, when out the corner of my eye I spotted my two sisters, eyes wide open, mouths wide open, taking in an event I was certain they would report the details of to Mom and Dad. I quickly made the decision that it was better to take a beating from a girl than to go home and suffer the consequences from my mom, and gave up my offensive position sitting on top of Jezebel.

She immediately began to beat the snot of me, much to the delight and applause of what must have been her entire family, as a crowd of her supporters gathered around and cheered her every blow.

When the ambush was over, my sisters came to my aid, helped up their defeated brother, and listened to his explanation for the beating ("It's not right to hit a girl") while we walked home.

The experience of being beaten up by a girl served me well when the initiation into country school began, as I already had an understanding of humility and how to handle pain.

I found the will to survive being hung by my ankles from the cottonwood tree in the southeast corner of the schoolyard; being forced to ride in between two swings with one foot on the seat of each then taken up by my fellow classmates to where the seats of the swings were even with the top bar of the swing set, and then told to jump off at the apex of the swing; and lastly by proving my own mettle by sneaking up close enough to hurl a rock at a hornet's nest and showing my agility by outrunning the resultant ensuing angry hornets without so much as one little sting.

Now, safe in the years that separate the past from the present, I can share that I have never really believed that my acceptance into this elite fraternity was in any way swayed by surviving the mass brawls that occurred every day during one of the recesses, or by receiving only minor cuts and nose bleeds during the rounds of games that we invented on a daily bases.

Games that we made up, created, and designed to ensure that we did not have any sissies in our classroom.

I am certain that my acceptance had little to do with the bravery I displayed by showing that I was not afraid to grab hold of the electric fence surrounding the alfalfa field that wrapped around the south and west borders of our school. I believe that it was definitely due to the fact that I proved, and removed all doubt, that I was not afraid of any of the teachers that tried to teach to us from school year to school year.

Some years it seemed that we went through more than one teacher. This must have created quite a problem for those farmers that sat on the school board; I would bet that teacher colleges all over the Midwest had to create a special program for understanding the psychology of the rural student.

Or maybe they didn't, for as the years go by it seems they have found that it was just easier to eliminate the country schools, as you sure don't see them around very much anymore.

The camaraderie of the students at District 14 was legendary. For over the years we had developed superiority unmatched in our ability to wreak havoc in the classroom. No matter what subject was being taught, no matter what grade of class being taught, we started getting requests to visit other schools for the sole purpose of sharing our secrets to other districts of farm kids.

It didn't matter if it was kindergarten reading time, third-grade math, sixth-grade social studies, or eighth-grade literature; any time was appropriate for the cunning and craftiness of our misguided behaviors.

Of course, we all knew that someday the fun would end. The only way to stop it from ending was to make sure that you did not get promoted into the next grade; an action that led to an entirely different set of actions we knew was better left unexplored.

For me, the end came when I was promoted into the eighth grade. That was when my entire class, that is, all two of us, were forced by our parents to transfer to school in town. Much to our surprise, we quickly became celebrities in town school and were welcomed with joyous celebration and open arms by those city kids when they saw that we had no desire to behave in the classroom.

We were accepted as equals by those city kids who put their faith in our abilities to put an end to the relentlessly boring ideas of what school was all about in the minds of the city schoolteacher.

Unfortunately, we all soon learned that reputation sometimes precedes punishment.

We also soon began to understand that continued education eventually leads to a place where discipline and maturity are essential if success is to be achieved!

But oh how we enjoyed those years of rebellious behavior. Like a badge of honor, I would fondly remember the time when the teacher just moved my desk to the front left-hand corner of the classroom and left me there for the remainder of the school year.

And then there was the time that we chased the teacher out of the schoolhouse and sent her packing down the road followed closely by those miner bees that we had brilliantly set free into the hollowed halls of that bastion of education.

Or those times that we older boys would take the sack lunches from the littler kids, take them up to the top of the cottonwood tree located in the back of the schoolyard, then from the summit of that tree throw potato chips down upon their pleas for justice as we ate their peanut butter sandwiches.

I admit that some days I am filled with remorse and regret for our behavior, but my remorse would not last long, as I would remember as if it were only yesterday our delight at coercing the new students into riding their bikes as fast as they could to the edge of the alfalfa fields west of the school, alfalfa fields covered with ice, as the colder nighttime temperatures had turned the previous day's snow thaw into a solid layer of frozen water.

As the unsuspecting new country kid sped toward the frozen alfalfa field we would holler at them to slam on the brakes of their bike just as they hit the edge of the ice, which would send them on an uncontrolled, chaotic slide over the ice patch.

Oh the sights and sounds they emitted when they where launched into an orbit that ended in a location dependent upon the speed at which they where traveling when they hit the edge of the ice patch!

That we survived is proof that God had a plan for each of us. That we still fondly remember those days lived in a simpler time, when all seemed right in the world, is proof enough for me that God had a plan all along. We were right where we were suppose to be, living and learning the difference between good and evil, having a good time being kids in times that seem to have faded away.

Chapter Fourteen
Sisters

*"But Dad, there were chickens in the road. Had
I not swerved into the ditch, I would have run
over and killed them."—Oldest Sister*

Sisters: if you ever had one, you understand how this one word can set your mind into a quiver of convulsive thought. If you had two or more, you understand how those thoughts could transform into uncontrollable anxiety.

Now combine the uncontrollable anxiety with the luck of being the youngest child in the family and you will begin to understand the basic foundations upon which my life was constructed, and how I ended up the way I did!

From the very moment in time that my brain was able to create memories, it seems that my sisters were always involved. Their primary involvement was in making certain that I saw things in the same light as did they. That I understood that they were in charge of each situation we found ourselves in, that they controlled my destiny.

From the time when they dressed me up as a little girl so I could play tea party with them, to the time that they tied me to a tree in front of the house we lived in before we moved to the farm, leaving me to go watch a neighbor's house burn down, I struggled to understand why God made it a necessity for me to have sisters.

The older sister was four years older than I was. She was the one that was generally responsible for conniving the other sister and me out of our hard-earned allowance, our rightful positions when in line for treats, a seat next to the window in the car, and our place in front of the TV to watch cartoons we wanted to watch. In fact, it was probably the older sister's fault that my other sister and I did not end up in positions of world fame and importance.

My other sister was only one year older than I was, and people always thought that we were twins. She was the one that would generally convince me that I should really be nice to the older sister. She was the one that generally negotiated the terms of the truce.

I will admit that my sisters did provide me with many hours of entertainment. They could make a seemingly endless summer day go much faster by providing me with an endless number of opportunities to be a brother.

Like the letters from the boyfriends that I could easily intercept from the mailbox located at the bottom of the hill on the road leading to our farmhouse. Letters that, once I had intercepted them, could be used to increase my position in bribing a sister in order to get my way. They understood that I had no fears about the consequences I might face if I opened these letters and read them out loud to the world.

They understood that I could climb most any tree in the yard, using it as a podium for my public announcements, in a matter of seconds. They understood that they could not climb any of those trees.

They also provided my dad with a number of opportunities to be their father.

It was with great delight that I would listen to the seemingly endless lectures prepared and delivered by my dad as he tried so desperately to deal with his daughters. Lectures that I must admit I have since borrowed when forced to administer justice to my own daughters.

It was the older sister that provided my other sister and me with the greatest lessons in what to try and what not to try with our parents. It seems that it is a natural responsibility of the oldest child in a multi-child family to test the waters of the world and provide information that can be used by the younger siblings of what to do, and what not to do!

Some of the greatest lessons my younger sister and I learned resulted from my older sister's inability to satisfy one of what I am sure are most parents' simplest requests: that request of being home by ten o'clock on school nights.

I learned that getting home by 10:30 could be dealt with by using relatively simple excuses that generally involved other friends, with only minor negotiation and/or simple clarification of facts. But coming home an hour beyond curfew required the ability to accept and deal with progressive punishment, as there wasn't an attorney on the planet that could justify such an intolerable act.

My older sister even taught me how to carefully use compassion for animals as a way to reduce the level of possible punishment for fairly severe mistakes. Like when she rolled the family car one night while on her way into town for cheerleader practice. "But Dad, there were chickens in the road. Had I not swerved into the ditch, I would have run over and killed them."

While this event taught me a new level of understanding toward the animal kingdom, the lesson evidently was lost on my mom. For very little time had gone by after this mishap when Mom showed a complete lack of compassion for animals by running right over one of the neighbor's pigs that had wandered out into the middle of the road she was driving on to get to town.

Of course, it was a pig, and I guess compassion is subjective when talking about fowl or swine. Of course, saying that the pig wandered out into the road is not really a true statement. To wander requires a mind seeking adventure, and I seriously doubt that any pig has ever ventured anywhere as the result of a purposeful thought. That the pig *wondered* into the road is more correct as I believe pigs are usually in the process of wondering about something.

Whether it is simply because of the closeness of our age or because of other things, my relationship with the sister that was one year older than me was much different from the relationship I had with my older sister.

When looking at photos taken of us back in those years I can see why most thought we must be twins. She and I did seem to have more in common. We shared a creative desire geared towards projects that had bigger rewards. I am surprised that neither of us turned into a world-class architect.

We organized and conducted the only Father's Day parade that ever ran on our farm. In fact, I would surmise that it was the only Father's Day parade ever held on any farm, complete with our originally designed, homemade float.

We also designed and constructed a number of clubhouses, one of which also provided entrepreneur opportunities. From it we sold valuable merchandize that we either raised in our own garden or made with our own talented hands.

From tree houses to dugouts, our architectural expertise brought laud and acclaim to us from many family members.

It also brought grumblings and complaints from my dad, and we noticed that whenever we were expecting company to visit our farm, if our latest design was visible to the guest it was quickly scheduled for demolition.

Each time we built a clubhouse, we would make an effort to spend an entire night in our completed project, a sort of very special sleepover meant as part of the initiation of each clubhouse. I do not remember that we successfully spent an entire night in any of our projects, though. Our mom would always sneak out into the darkness of the middle of the night and start making ghost-like noises in an effort to drive us back into the safety of our bedrooms in the farmhouse.

My sisters also seemed to always have the upper hand in our sister-brother relationship, primarily because of that darn one-room country school we attended. It was hard to keep my mischief at school a secret to our parents, what with the two sisters knowing all about everything I did, as they attended the same school. Silly me!

Of course, I took full advantage of the one year I was in country school without them, as they had both been promoted to town school.

Looking back at those wonderful years on the farm helps me to understand that I do enjoy a special bond with my sisters, a bond forged by the trials and tribulations of farm life.

Chapter Fifteen
The State Fair

"Me and the boy are going over to women's
lingerie!"—Grandpa Farmer

The end of summer was always eagerly anticipated by our family. Each August our family would make the journey to our state's capital city in order to participate in and enjoy the state fair.

The participating part was always played by my sisters, as each year they would honor their commitment to the local 4-H chapter, competing in local competition for the right to compete at the state fair. The enjoyment role was clearly the role played by myself, as my only commitment was to eat as many foot-long hot dogs as I could in the short time we were at the fair.

The competitions that my sisters took part in where called demonstrations. Not the kind of demonstrations that brought out the riot police, but demonstrations on such useful things as cooking pizza or making pastries, or activities like the proper way to exercise, how to sew, knit, or make scrapbooks.

You see, you had to compete for the right to go to the state fair in the competitions held at the local county fair. The various classifications of demonstrations, or items baked, were then judged by a fair and impartial panel of judges, and those that received a purple ribbon won the honor of going to the state fair competition.

At least that is how I remember it!

For me the county fairs and the state fair had a much easier explanation of purpose: a time for rest, relaxation, and adventure. Although these annual journeys to the state capital did not require any formal commitments from me, I did make a commitment to climb around on all the new farm equipment and, if I haven't mentioned it, to eat as many foot-long hot dogs complete with onions, ketchup, mustard, and relish as I could.

For my sisters, the state fair process would start at the beginning of each summer. The process started with many hours of thought about what demonstration activity would have the best chance of winning the right to advance to the state fair, or by selecting the recipe that would yield a result that received the approval of the local judges at the county fair for submission to those judges at the state level.

I was never able to understand, even when given lengthy explanations to my inquires, how a frosted lemon pound cake could be baked, placed on a Styrofoam plate, covered with clear wrap, and submitted for judging at the county level the first week of August and maintain the flavor and texture needed to be fairly judged at the state level almost a month later.

Nevertheless, my sisters seemed to understand what it took, as each year they earned the right not only to compete at the state fair with their well-rehearsed demonstrations, but also to exhibit various cookies, cakes, and pastries.

I am certain that my first thoughts about the fairness of this world came from those days of my sisters' preparations for the county and state fairs. I was amazed that the younger of the two sisters could get anything past the local judges without the need to transport them to the local hospital, or at least induce vomiting to save them from possible fatal poisoning.

It was a well-known fact in our family that my older sister was a pretty fair cook, but the younger of the two sisters' knowledge of the proper kitchen technique was somewhat suspect, fueled by actions such as when she put leftover oatmeal into the refrigerator so that we could enjoy it the next day.

My mom and older sister spent a lot of time helping middle child master the art of boiling water and taught her the scientific reasons that required you to keep ice cream in the freezer. The younger of the two sisters was pretty smart. I guess that cooking wasn't a big enough challenge for her. It was amazing the way she could cook up things that would have no taste.

The art of perfecting their chosen recipes started each year in the later weeks of May, running through June and July, and cumulating with that final masterpiece created for submission to the county fair judges usually the first week of August.

That period of time in between was full of ample opportunity for my grandpa, Dad, Yogi, and I to be the guinea pigs in tasting the results of each cooking session's labor.

"Let the boy eat it first, he can eat anything," my grandpa would proclaim when the time for eating the samples was at hand. "Yeah, and if it kills him then we will know better than to try it," I'm certain Yogi would chime in.

My dad seemed to always be conveniently sitting on the tractor out in the field during most of these tasting sessions, but I would admit that I generally enjoyed being asked to sample the results of each recipe. Yogi was always appreciative; each effort was an award-winner in his opinion.

For Yogi and me it was the demonstrations that provided the most entertainment. The demonstrations required that my sisters step out into an area in which they had little or no knowledge in if they wanted to truly have a shot at competing on a state level.

If I were to put together a top-ten list of the all-time favorite sister demonstrations, there is little doubt that the list would be headed by the year the younger of my two sisters and her friend chose the topic of pizza making as that which would lead them to the Promised Land of the state fair. Not only was it okay with Yogi and me that we would be eating an increased number of pizzas in the months leading up to the county fair, but we also greatly anticipated my sister's introduction into that world of gas appliances.

In order to bake each pizza, she would need to learn how to light our farm's gas oven, an oven that could cause even my grandma to utter words that we could not understand.

This search for the perfect pizza started with a bang one Monday morning in June as my sister and her best friend began to learn the art of lighting an oven fueled by propane gas.

My dad, my dog, Yogi, and I had just settled into the task of making new dams for the upcoming irrigation season. We had all the necessary supplies spread out on the ground on the west side of the barn and had just begun to develop a rhythm to hasten the assembly of each dam, when the quiet of the morning air was interrupted with a loud explosion, its point of ignition coming from the area of the farmhouse in which the kitchen was located.

The explosion sent birds flying in every direction, scaring them in such a manner that they did not return for days.

The sound and suddenness of the explosion was such that Yogi was lifted about two feet off the ground, maintaining that position he frequently used while licking and cleaning his front paws, which were politely crossed in front of him.

The explosion caused my dad to miss the center of the six-foot-long piece of two-by-two with the electric drill that he was using to drill holes for the ropes that would be used to support the plastic that would become the working portion of each dam, which gave cause for that moment right after the explosion to be filled with his wealth of unmentionable words that he stored up for times such as this.

The explosion and my dad's exaltations were followed by the panicked exit from the kitchen of those two wannabe award-winning chefs, complete with screams of varying degrees.

Of course, for Yogi and me it was hard to resist the urge to run as fast as we could for the house in order to be first on the scene to survey the damage; however, it was easier to resist this urge when we got a closer look at the alterations that the blast had made to the outward appearance of the pizza chefs.

Each of them was sporting added evidence that something was amiss in the form of singed hairs on their heads, arms, and eyebrows on top of their seemingly two-times-larger eyes.

The things you see when you don't have a camera. The lack of eyebrows and arm hair alone on these two future brides was sufficient cause for Yogi to roll on the ground in convulsive joy. I did my best to keep his exuberance down to a level to which he would be able to repair any damage this was inflicting on that relationship he enjoyed with my sister, but there was no one in attendance that could help me out with this same type of looking after.

I sure she was greatly relieved by my reassurance that you can't get lockjaw from burns, that her hair would grow back, and that I wouldn't tell anyone about what had happened.

The damage to the kitchen was minimal, the hair on the bakers' heads, faces, and arms would eventually return, but the amount of time that would be required for a brother to forget about a moment such as this is to this day still undetermined.

I don't even remember if this particular demonstration made it to state fair. All I know for certain is that it ranks right up at the top of those things I remember about my sisters and their involvement in 4-H.

The actual process of traveling to, attending, and then traveling home from the state fair was always a highlight of the year. Anytime we packed suitcases and traveled to a location that required a stay in a hotel was a highlight.

My dad and I would typically spend one day at the fair wandering through the farm equipment exhibits and another full day milling about the animal barns. Of course, we had to reserve time to watch the sisters in their moment of glory at the 4-H demonstration building.

It took another day each for the numerous exhibit halls and the dirt track stock car races and tractor pulls, with yet another day reserved for shopping the downtown area of our wonderful capital city.

Of course, there were also the rides at the carnival that was set up each year at the fair, and did I mention the eating of foot-long hot dogs complete with onions, mustard, ketchup, and relish?

I did not care too much for the shopping, but sometimes shopping had its rewards, especially when Granddad Farmer happened to go along. The grandparents did not normally go with us each year to the state fair, but when they did go, their presence would always add a dimension of surprise to the trip.

On our last day in the city the family would invariably end up rendezvousing in one of the numerous department stores in the capital city's downtown area. This would give the womenfolk a chance to shop for clothes before we started our journey home. I remember the time my granddad grabbed me by the arm and proclaimed to the rest of the family, "Me and the boy are going over to women's lingerie!"

We would actually end up seated comfortably at the fountain bar of the closest drug store, sipping on one last malt or soda before we headed back to the real world on the farm.

Those annual journeys to the state fair were indeed a celebration of a life lived on the family farm; a time now lived in the confines of my mind, whenever I'm searching for a better place, in a better time, where simple things seemed to be just fine.

Chapter Sixteen

Mom

*"Even my dog, Yogi, understood the essential necessity
of keeping within the good graces of my mom, she from
which all table scraps flowed."—Words of Wisdom*

Can anyone really remember that exact moment in their life when they first met Mom, eye to eye?

Does there exist on this earth anyone who would be able to compile a list of the feelings and emotions created by the bond that we have developed with our moms? Is it possible that all of the fundamental characteristics that define our personalities and instincts are a result of those tender moments that we shared in our lives with the woman who delivered us into this life?

I'm not able to say that I can remember a time when I thought my dad was the only other person on earth, or that without my sisters I would not be able to find the keys held to my future. But your mom … I think most of us would agree that Mom was like reaching home base when playing tag. She was the city of refuge we all sought out when we needed to escape the avenger of those deeds or fears that are a part of this life.

I recall with great clarity the many moments in my life, prior to when God gave me a wife of my own, that Mom was that central figure from which I thought all things that brought joy and peace to my life would flow.

Even my dog, Yogi, understood the essential necessity of keeping within the good graces of my mom, she from which all table scraps flowed.

I recall when my mom discovered that I didn't like beats; I remember her picking herself up off the floor, having slipped on the wet noodles that had been placed there as a result of my unwillingness to eat beats.

Mom proceeded to chase me all over the house, as she proclaimed, "I have had enough!

Lucky to escape her wrath, I found myself well hid in the same closet that harbored those gifts from Santa each Christmas. Suddenly understanding that no good could possible come from the choice I had made to hide in this closet, and, discovering within me a desire of wanting to survive the complex actions of a mother I could still hear searching for me, I went back to the kitchen to turn myself in.

Arriving in the kitchen I was suddenly confronted by that warm loving feeling that could only be generated in a heart as compassionate as the one that beat inside the women who was determined to see that I left the world she had brought me into on good terms.

Fearing the pain that was destined to be felt emanating from my rear end, I covered my butt with my hands knowing the moment of truth that was about to come as mom turned from cleaning the food on the floor and saw me standing next to the table. A table that was still bearing a bowl full of beats that started this whole mess.

It could have been compassion, sprinkled with a little bit of mercy, but more than likely it was the knowledge that I would be a better kid when this was over then I was when I walked into the room. A knowledge that would help me to make it through yet another of those lessons that mom taught on a daily bases.

It was always really hard to keep myself from becoming involved in anything that led to adventure while growing up on our farm. When the flesh prevailed and you found yourself in the middle of a scene that you knew would end up with some form of discipline, it was mom's discipline that you feared the most.

For me it was not so much the actual act of discipline that my mom would have to wield that I feared, it was more the look of disappointment I saw on her face that I would lament.

My mom was a petite woman even in the prime of her adult life, but the speed with which she could raise her hand to administer the consequences of my inability to follow her direction still gives me the shivers.

I don't recall that there was anything that my mom couldn't do. She was always available to play the piano for the country school when we prepared for the annual school play or rehearsed for the annual town school activity day's singing competition.

Her desserts were easily identified whenever attending one of the many church potlucks or multiple-family cookouts, desserts that always seemed to be gone before any of the other desserts.

In those rare moments when you could actually get Mom to become a participant in any type of game, she exhibited athletic coordination that led you to believe that, had she really wanted to, she could have been a world-class athlete.

Mom showed her competitive spirit whenever she took up the position of sports fan at one of the local high school sporting events or when watching our state's beloved college football team. Her support of her son's endeavors on the field of competition was without compromise and at times somewhat embarrassing.

She displayed the same loyal support for my sisters at the events that they participated in, events that in those days clearly helped to define the difference between boys and girls. She was as proud of my sister's performance in Job's Daughters or 4-H as she was of her son's touchdowns, races won, or shots made in basketball.

A farm kid's need for food was a primary argument to sway favor to your mom. When you smelled the aroma of a fresh-baked apple pie carried with the breeze while herding cows to the barn from the winter cornfields, or heard the joyful pealing of that little dinner bell she rang to summon the family into another one of her roast beef dinners, the balance sheet was set to be swayed in the favor of mom.

When you needed help with school work or a chore, or a sister needed help understanding the actions of her brother, it was Mom that was always ready to jump in and help.

I'm certain that I have never been able to justifiably explain my feelings towards a mom that was always ready to drop everything for her kids. I know that I have not apologized for all those wonderfully foolish things I did as a boy, but perhaps she will be able to read this chapter, and then she will understand how important she was and still is to the little boy she used to hold in her arms.

Chapter Seventeen
Fishing with Dad

*"Why the hell would I want to be bothered by some
stupid fish when I want to take a nap?"—Dad*

Fishing could become an addiction for me. An addiction fueled by the need to experience the fulfillment and the realization of the catch. A realization that is not complete unless you are actually able to take the fish off the hook after the successful fight. For me, fishing grew past the mark that makes it a hobby, and it became one of those things that created a passion in my mind.

Fishing was an activity that I was introduced to at an early age. Growing up on the farm, I learned very early on about the true meaning of a hard day's work. A day on the farm started at o'dark thirty each morning, and ended when Mom would finally ring the supper bell. That is, it ended if you were able to hear the sound created by that wonderful little bell.

Many a cold supper was the result of working aboard a tractor, the calling of the supper bell going unheard over the powerful drone of a tractor's diesel engine.

Few things could equal that blissful feeling provided by the nervous system of your tired body when its ear heard that cue, the ringing of that wonderful bell, releasing you from another hard day's work.

One sound that did compete with the frequency that emitted from that bell was the sound of Dad's voice announcing as only he could, "Let's go fishing tomorrow."

My dad had a great work ethic. He believed that a job started could be finished in the same day, no matter what the scope of work was that the job entailed. If it required that a few more hours be put into the day, so be it.

The many long days worked those years on our little farm provided for me in my adult life an appreciation for the peace and renewal of spirit that can be found in the sport of fishing.

It seemed that on the farm you rarely had the advantage of being able to think about what to do next. More times than not a storm was on the way, the hay needed to be put up before the rain hit, or the corn needed to be picked before the first snow.

Farming was an activity in which you found reward by making decisions on your feet. I found it very hard to change from this philosophy when later in life I became involved in a corporate world that many times said, "You need to be patient, things don't always happen overnight." I am certain that most of the business executives of this day and age would have starved to death as farmers!

I guess it was a combination of these two worlds that created within me a philosophy that says when it is time to work, work hard; when it is time to play, play hard; and when it comes time to fish, fish hard—but expect to catch fish.

Our fishing trips took form in one of three ways: a short drive down to the river for some serious catfishing, a longer drive to one of the many lakes within an hour's drive of our farm, or the decree that the entire family was going camping, which meant a trip for the whole family to one of the state parks, which were always next to a lake.

My sisters would always protest the latter decree that called for the family camping trip. I don't know why we had to take sisters along on these trips. If they wanted to stay home then leave them. They would only get in the way, especially when they caught more fish than I did, which, by the way, was not very often.

The trips down to the river for some serious catfishin' usually resulted in an accompanying nap for both Yogi and my dad. Come to think of it, so did the fishing trips to the nearest lake or the family camping/ fishing trips.

My dad could be very selfish with his time when fishing. He only allotted so much time for the fish to have an opportunity to mess with his idea of relaxation. Generally, he would settle into taking his nap, relying on a built-in instinct that would automatically wake him up the minute I caught a fish, declaring with his boisterous voice that "it was now time to let the fishing begin."

He would also always make sure that we took some food along with us on any fishing trip. You never knew when hunger might try to get in the way of fishing. I remember one of his favorite fishing snacks was to take a piece of bologna and put it on top of a cinnamon roll.

It seemed to me that some of the catfish bait we used when fishing the river would be better tasting than that. But then, the catfish bait that my dad and I concocted was so toxic that you had to wear leather gloves when putting it on your hook. You had to clean any fish you caught immediately after you got it off of the hook, or the bait would taint the taste of the fish.

My dad was also careful to teach me the art of prioritizing when placed into a situation that required multitasking. He did this by cleverly putting nothing on his fishing line but a bare hook and a bobber, the bobber being placed less than six inches from the bare hook. He would then cast this combination less than a foot from the boat or shoreline before putting his feet up in preparation for a few zzzzzz's.

When I would question him about the effectiveness of this tactic in catching fish, he would look at me as if he could not believe just how foolish a son he had raised. "Why the hell would I want to be bothered by some stupid fish when I want to take a nap?" was his sharp reply.

My favorite memory of our many fishing trips together actually had nothing to do with catching fish. Years later I realized that this was one of those rare moments when I was allowed to witness just how rare and original my dad was.

It was a moment in time that only a loving God could place in the relationship between a father and his son, a moment when the dad taught his son to understand that sovereign right we all have to enjoy the beautiful earth that He placed us on to live.

It was a beautiful spring morning at one of our local lakes. The sun was still hiding just below the eastern sky, the birds were singing songs that only an all-knowing God could teach, and we had just settled in for a morning of bluegill fishing.

Suddenly, the quiet morning air was disrupted by the rattling noises that can only accompany a car that is not happy about being used. The kind of car that is driven by a city slicker, a city slicker that is not too concerned about how his lifestyle might effect others.

A city slicker who had no idea how his life was about to change that day as he came driving up next to the lake in his early 1960s clunker. He backed the sputtering pile of junk up to the very edge of the lake, turned off the engine, got out, and opened up his trunk, pulling out a lawn chair and a radio. He unfolded his lawn chair, sat down, and turned the radio on to a station broadcasting somewhere out of the state of Missouri. He also made sure that he set the volume at a level that would ensure that anyone within two miles of our location could hear the broadcast.

There was suddenly a feeling in the morning's air like the quiet that sometimes occurs before the storm, or that moment of peace that exists within the eye of a hurricane. Time suddenly seemed to stop. It quickly became obvious, at least to me, that I about to witness an act that would forever change someone's perception of what fishing was all about!

After less than two minutes of listening to that radio broadcasting from somewhere out of the state Missouri, Dad looked at me with that same look of his that I thought he had reserved for only those moments when I brought home a report card with an F on it. He got up from his special tree stump, that special tree stump that dad always seemed to find no matter where we went fishing, and walked over to the unsuspecting city slicker, making certain that his six-foot-four-inch frame, which by the way carried a good 230 pounds of pure, hard-working farmer muscle, would intimidate as much as it possibly could.

As he approached the city slicker's location, the sky suddenly clouded over and music could be heard coming from nowhere, music that I would years later hear again as the theme song to a movie about wars fought in galaxies far, far away.

I knew I was about to witness a moment that I would want to remember forever in that motion-picture-camera mind that the good Lord gave us for the preserving of memories such as these.

When Dad got to where the city slicker was sitting, he reached down and grabbed that radio right in the middle of the hog belly futures, and in one fluid motion sent that broadcast from somewhere in Missouri on a trajectory that created a splashdown a good thirty feet from the shoreline.

The last sound you heard broadcast through the little speakers on the radio broadcast from somewhere in the state of Missouri was accompanied by a large splash as it hit the water to the musical jingle created by the advertising team of that station somewhere in Missouri, "This ... is ... K ... W ... O ... bubbley ... OOOHHH ... bbbbuubbuuulll yeeuuuooooouuurrpppp...."

His mission accomplished, Dad left the gentleman with a glare that, though I couldn't see it, generated a response from that city slicker that left me in no doubt that this gentlemen from the city had a newfound respect for the natural beauty, peace, and quiet of the great outdoors.

He didn't budge an inch from his plastic, woven lawn chair the rest of the time we were there!

We caught a lot of fish, he caught a lot of quiet time, and I had a memory that to this day receives a lot of doubtful looks from those to whom I fondly recall that morning.

CHAPTER EIGHTEEN
THE WEEK AT THE LAKE

*"... one of the beautiful things about fishing is that you
can sit in one spot for hours, staring out into space,
fishing pole in hand, and anyone that observes you
will see nothing wrong with you."—Boy on Fishing*

Towards the end of each summer, when the irrigation season was over, when state and county fair photos had been properly filed away into the family's photo album, when the work of summer seemed to have each member of the family at that point were sanity was slipping fast, we would take a trip into one of the neighboring states for a week of relaxation and, for me, a week of fishing.

In the years that we had a possibility for a bumper crop, my parents would allow us to spend two weeks at a cabin on a lake. To this young farm kid, two weeks at a lake for the express purpose of fishing had to be the closest thing imaginable to heaven on earth.

Whether one week or two, it didn't matter to me. And while the rest of the family formulated plans for other activities, my one-track mind could only concentrate on fishing each and every moment of each and every day.

The lake that we went to was a good day's drive from our farm. Each year we always seemed to end up in the same cabin, and the neighboring cabins always seemed to have the same families staying in them. I suppose this was no accident and somehow had been made possible by the careful planning of each family's mom.

No matter, the schemes required to make this trip possible, the amount of driving time required to reach the destination, and the opportunity to start and end each day sitting on the shoreline of a lake, fishing, was more than I could ask for.

This was the culminating event of the summer, the reward at the end of the rainbow, a journey that each year would yield that elusive treasure searched for in the dreams I dreamed at night.

Of course, my sisters would each voice their displeasure at the potential of wasting another year's worth of vacation at some stupid lake when we could just as easily go to any city in any state and shop, an argument that thankfully fell on the deaf ears of my parents.

The cabin we stayed in had two bedrooms and either a couch that made into a bed or a rollaway bed conveniently folded up and placed in the corner of the kitchen/living room. It was always determined that I would be the one that did not get a bedroom, a decision that fell right into my own schemes, as I was always up before the first light of day to sneak out without disturbing the rest of the family and make my way to one of my favorite spots, sitting out on the end of the boat dock, fishing pole in hand, living out my dreams, and providing fish for breakfast.

It was really cool to be out on that dock each morning to watch the nighttime sky turn into the first light of morning, to witness the sky change from a starlit canvas into a sunlight-washed panorama of every shade of blue, with clouds thrown in for contrast.

I was always fascinated by the fresh, clear waters of the lakes in the northern part of the country, and the opportunity that they provided for a kid to observe the rituals created by fish in determining which one of them was going to have the honor of risking its all, darting from the school in an effort to grab the minnow being sacrificed on the hook that was running from the reel that was on my fishing pole.

I had always thought fish acted out of instinct when carelessly grabbing hold of whatever offering a fisherman had at the end of their line. But those clear, cool waters of the northern lake revealed an activity that appeared to be dictated by centuries of fish school logic.

The fish I was trying to catch were called yellow perch. Watching these fish roam the clear waters of this northern lake revealed that they stayed in groups, packs, or, in fisherman terms, schools. When the school would come upon an unsuspecting minnow, they would circle around it in the same fashion that the attacking plains tribes would surround the wagons that they intended to attack in those Westerns you see on television.

I decided that the purpose of this formation surrounding the unsuspecting minnow was to ensure that it could not get away from the school before one of its members swooped in and devoured the poor, unsuspecting bait fish.

I was never able to figure out how these fish determined which of them was going to be the lucky fish that got to eat the prey. I decided it was probably something similar to those methods we used at our country school to determine who gets to be it, or when my sisters and I determined who got the last scoop of ice cream from the homemade ice cream freezer on a hot summer day. That ritual taught to all kids no matter where they live on this earth: rock, paper, scissors!

Fishing gives the fisherman ample opportunity for using his brain. That process, thinking, is a mental process that can absolutely ruin the sport. I've seen fisherman that spend all their time thinking and none of their time realizing the catch.

I have always thought that one of the beautiful things about fishing is that you can sit in one spot for hours, staring out into space, fishing pole in hand, and anyone that observes you will see nothing wrong with you. Just try sitting anywhere else with a fishing pole in your hand, not moving for hours, staring into space, and watch how quickly the men come to take you away.

All I really cared to see was that flash of light reflecting off the scales of a fish that is making the move to take the bait, followed by the quick submersion of the bobber that was attached to the same line as the hook and minnow.

The deftness with which I could set the hook on a fish was undoubtedly as professional as any you might witness by other fisherman. It was a rare fish that could escape becoming the newest addition to my always-getting-fuller fish stringer.

Fishing from the dock also gave me an opportunity to sharpen my rock-skipping abilities. Of course, this required that I divide my attention between watching the bobber on my line and the process of selecting those flat rocks required for this art. Any rock side-armed onto the smooth surface of the lake that did not skip at least three skips was deemed an illegal throw, at least in the official rules of all things that were conveniently stored within the confines of my own vast thoughts.

I recall once or twice that my rock-skipping activities would be interrupted by the discovery that my fishing pole was no longer laying on the end of the dock where I left it. This mystery was quickly solved when I would spot the pole lying at the bottom of the lake just in front of the dock.

Which led to the discovery of just how cold that clear water in those northern lakes is! Especially when you stripped off your clothes and experienced the early morning cold and wetness as you jumped in to retrieve your fishing gear.

Each trip to the lake would include a day or two when my dad would pay for the rental of a boat and motor, which allowed him and me the opportunity to troll the lake in search of bigger fish.

I would dream about setting the hook and fighting a great big northern pike or one of those big old muskellunge trophy fish that roamed the waters of that lake, a dream that has only been partially fulfilled as the musky has eluded me still.

Going out in the boat to troll for fish was exciting, but it also created an uneasy feeling for me each year, as I knew that eventually my dad was going to hook a fish and actually reel it in all the way up to the boat. This would require that someone net the fish, and as I was the only other one in the boat, the act of netting was up to me.

The process of netting a fish that your dad had skillfully hooked and maneuvered up to the boat was a process that only had two possible conclusions. Either the fish ended up in the boat or the fish ended up swimming off back into the lake, leaving you in the boat with an unhappy fisherdad; thus, the anxiety.

More than once my dad's catch would somehow evade my net and jump from the hook just as it was brought to the side of our boat. I did not enjoy those looks of disdain from my dad, looks that brought with them some of the same words I had associated with broken-down corn pickers and mad sows that would not get into the truck.

But Dad would always calm down and replace those looks with smiles and words of encouragement: "He wasn't big enough anyway. I let him get away so that we can come back next year and catch a bigger fish."

He would then crank up the motor and head for another of my favorite fishing holes, one that was right below a railroad trestle on the southeast end of the lake.

We would tie off the boat to one of the beams that supported the trestle and have a great time catching whatever would bite until the late hours of the afternoon began to give way to the early hours of evening.

The weeks at the lake always seemed to go by so fast. The picnics, the games of horseshoes, the swimming at the beach, even the time spent with my sisters is fondly remembered as a week when you truly did experience rest and your troubles became things of the past.

CHAPTER NINETEEN
BB GUNS AND SANTA CLAUS

"To John, From Santa"—from the tag on a present

I was one of those kids that held dearly to the belief that Santa Claus was as real as you and me. It was a belief that was founded in greed, in a desire to get as many Christmas presents as I could.

A BB gun played a major role in the series of events that eventually led me out of that make-believe world I was living in and into the far more serious world in which you no longer received a gift from Santa Claus.

It was my very first gun that started me down the path that would eventually force me to grow up. It was my very first BB gun that began the avalanche of lessons and tests that would separate me from the land of childhood fantasy where the Tooth Fairy, the Easter Bunny, and Santa Claus resided.

It was a path leading to the world of adulthood that strangely enough had its beginning in the only bathroom that existed in our family farmhouse.

You see, the bathroom in our family's farmhouse was located adjacent to a closet that doubled as a secret passage, one that would allow me to sneak out of my bedroom whenever my parents decided that I should be confined to it.

It was a rather large closet that doubled as a storage area for suitcases and boxes full of stuff. My parents had evidently thought that this closet was invisible to kids, as it was also one of their favorite hiding places for those gifts that needed hiding in the weeks that led up to Christmas Day.

It was about three weeks prior to the Christmas that coincided with my maturing to that age when you are deemed old enough to own your very first BB gun. This particular year I was not even in the hunt for Christmas gifts yet, as it was still too early in the Christmas season. I was simply sitting upon the toilet seat answering nature's call, when my boredom with this menial task led my eyes to the very top shelf of that closet that created that secret passage from my sometimes bedroom prison. On that top shelf sat a box that said in big bold letters BB Gun!

I guess Mom and Dad thought that I must be pretty stupid. Or maybe they didn't think I paid much attention to things. I doubt that they understood the obligation that all kids have to each other to try and find as many Christmas gifts as possible that parents hide in the house before Christmas Day rolled around.

You would think that on a farm with so many different buildings the parents would have unlimited opportunities to successfully hide the kids' presents! You would think that my sisters and I would find it very difficult to locate our gifts, especially on our farm, as my grandparents lived in a separate trailer house not fifteen feet from the farmhouse my immediate family occupied. You would think that, wouldn't you?

The discovery of this gift made those weeks leading up to Christmas Day extremely long.

When those long and difficult days did finally pass, my anticipation was further delayed by one of those Christmas morning rituals the parents had created designed to enhance those 8mm films that my uncle always took. My parents used to line my sisters and I up, according to height, and parade us out into the living room, where the Christmas tree was located as my uncle was panning the room with his 8mm movie camera, filming the event for the enjoyment of future generations.

The family's Christmas tree was always the center of a couple of other Christmastime rituals, one of which was that the entire family had to go and select the tree. One year we all hiked down to the river near our farm and cut down a cedar tree, dragged it back to the house, and decorated it with that pride that comes with knowing you didn't spend any hard-earned money on the tree.

That cedar tree began to smell up the house a few days later, and I recall hearing a commotion one night in the living room. I got up and made it to the living room just in time to see my dad, uttering words about stinking cedar trees, open the front door and toss the tree, decorations and all, out onto the front yard while he was clad in nothing but his underwear.

Another ritual was for the family to parade out to the tree each night after supper and sing Christmas carols, ending each night's caroling with "The Christmas Tree Song."

On this fateful Christmas morning, all rituals finally complete, I had to wait until the last presents where distributed before I got to unwrap the gift that I knew was coming. When at last my mom handed me the irregularly shaped package wrapped in paper adorned with Santas and candy canes, the trauma began.

For there, written on the tag that was taped to the wrapping paper, written in plain English for all to see, were the words, "To John, From Santa"!

My mind raced at the implications of the horrifying information contained on this innocent gift tag. "From Santa"? What, had the Jolly Bearded One dropped the gift off early one fall day when he happened to be in the neighborhood?

Was this an evil trick being carried out by my sisters with my parents' knowledge?

Was the entire world going to hell all around me, and there was nothing I could do about it?

Looking back on this moment in time, I think it was when I first understood how to call upon those experiences and abilities gained from growing up on a farm to handle any situation you might confront.

I chose a lesson that I had learned from my faithful companion Yogi and made a quick decision to play dumb, not letting on that I had seen this gift in the secret passageway many weeks ago. This was the obvious choice to make, as I was certain that should I reveal the truth that I knew who this gift was really from, I would jeopardize future gifts that would surely keep coming from Santa and his little elves. It was a sound strategy.

Better yet, it worked as in the years that proceeded from that moment when I was made a member of the gun owner's society: the gifts from Santa did indeed continue to come.

I was quick in proving my abilities to safely handle a BB gun, and the years of BB gun ownership went by without major dilemma, except for the time I accidentally discharged the weapon at some innocent barn windows. And a couple of times when I was admonished by my parents to stop shooting at the chickens, as it was having a negative effect on their abilities to lay eggs.

I was actually a pretty decent shot with the BB gun and was rewarded for my responsible behavior by receiving a more powerful .22 caliber pellet gun for Christmas two years later. From Santa, of course!

The more powerful CO_2 cartridge–powered pellet gun provided this farm kid with greater opportunities to disprove his maturity. And it seemed that I was able to discover most of those opportunities.

Barn windows had to be my most frequent downfall. I believe that the glass used to make barn windows must contain some sort of material that attracted lead fired from a rifle.

The pellet gun ammo also seemed to be attracted to some protected species of birds, or at least they were species of birds protected by my parents. But I was always very careful not to shoot my sisters, my friends, or, more important, myself.

The other half of my class at District 14 lived on a farm that was a couple of miles from ours, a couple of miles if you walked along the gravel road; it was only one and a half miles as the crow flies.

Our class was able to go on many field trips together since him and me were the only two in it. Of course, none of these field trips had anything to do with school. But each of them did teach us a lot about nature, and about ourselves.

We had many opportunities as kids to meet at various locations in between our two farms for hours of hunting and exploring. Hunting that yielded trophies that he and I vowed never to discuss with any adults.

I doubt that the world has ever been in any more danger than it was potentially in when my classmate and I reached that age that brought with it our parents' permission to hunt with shotguns and high-caliber rifles.

Yogi certainly understood as he wisely would go in the other direction whenever my classmate and I set off on one of our journeys that included our guns.

We made certain to maintain that oath of secrecy that our entire class had vowed when we were but young lads wielding BB guns in an effort to ensure that we would never be forced to surrender our arms.

We particularly made a favorable impression on our parents one summer when we showed promise as veterinary students, nursing back to health an injured pigeon we came upon on one of our class field trips.

Our parents seemed to be impressed by the compassion we showed in rescuing a member of the great outdoors and of our commitment to daily treat its wounds until the day came when we carried it off into the woods in its little cage to release it back into the wilds of nature.

We were always glad that our parents didn't take a closer look at the wounds suffered by that pigeon. Wounds we felt obligated to treat, as they had been created by a gunshot that was aimed at a more meaningful target. We could not believe how the carefully aimed shot could ricochet off my friend's dad's steel machine shed roof and into the wing of that poor in-the-wrong-place-at-the-wrong-time pigeon.

At the time of this unfortunate incident, we had both agreed that luck was with us, as the errant ricochet could have put a hole in the machine shed roof, or worse, found its way into some cattle that grazed in the field adjacent to the shed.

Of course, the fate of that successfully treated pigeon as it flew back into the wilds from the cage in which it had been nursed back to health, will forever remain untold to the rest of the world. It was a fate that was better left to the hard-to-understand confines of the minds that made up the membership of our country school class.

Our parents agreed that while few things seemed to get our full attention, the ownership of guns seemed to place us into an atmosphere in which we thrived. Actually, they were right, as gun ownership gave an opportunity to understand and demonstrate a level of care and maturity that we have fallen back on many times.

An understanding taught us that when guns were involved, if we had any hope of surviving to see the light of the next day, proper care, diligence, and respect was required.

It was an understanding that we knew came from witnessing the results of the power generated by gunpowder packed into a shell.

Ultimately, our ability to choose wisely was greatly enhanced from those times we spent hunting. Those many hunting trips that taught us the wisdom needed to weigh potential gain against possible damage, which led to a respect for life and an understanding of the finality of death.

CHAPTER TWENTY
THE END OF A LIFESTYLE

*"Well now, boy, about time you finally decided to
get down to business."—Grandpa Farmer*

Those years lived on the farm have long ago blended into memories
that when recalled are today as sweet as the best-tasting food your
mouth has ever tasted. I remember listening to many conversations
held those last few years on the farm, when my grandparents talked
about how farm life was not like it used to be.

I would guess that the rest of my family knew that the days of the family
farm would not last forever, but I could not imagine living anywhere
else when I was a kid.

While 180 acres was indeed more than enough land for the farm kid
to find excitement and adventure, it was not enough land for a family
to generate the income needed in providing the means for extravagant
purchases such as new tractors and better farm equipment, let alone
those necessary purchases such as feed for the animals, seed for the
crops, a college education for three kids, or even those things you could
not raise such as a brand-new pair of jeans.

My parents tried to make the farm work out. They both took on what
others in the world would call "real jobs" in order to be able to afford
our farming habit. Dad was forced to fall back on his education and
resume his career as a teacher at the local high school. Mom took on a
second job as a clerk at the county extension office.

Don't interpret this as whining; it's not as if we lived a life of poverty. In fact, our family lived a lifestyle on the farm that was far from one of poverty.

Each year we selected the best from our small farm's new crop of calves, feeding them the corn from our fields and yielding some of the best beef you could ever place on a plate.

I remember the amazement of my California-raised wife when I took her back home to the farm for a visit, amazement generated by the fact she found that my accounts of eating T-bone steaks without the aid of a knife were true. A T-bone so big that it required its own plate; that is, if you wanted to eat the vegetables from the family garden that went along with a typical steak dinner.

Each year our freezer could not contain the bounty of the harvest from our little farm. In fact, we had to rent freezer space from the local butcher shop in town in order to contain the harvest of meat, poultry, and frozen vegetables that our farm yielded.

The family garden was so large that it was located in two places. The garden plot south of the farmhouse was primarily for tomatoes and potatoes. The garden east of the house grew sweet corn, peas, beans, eggplant, cucumbers, lettuce, radishes, and lots of other vegetables in quantities large enough to last us from season to season.

In between these two garden plots stood an apple tree and two cherry trees, which served to provide the foundation for a pie-eating habit that I still maintain today. Those trees also accounted for many of the stomachaches I experienced each summer.

We grew enough sweet corn each year that we could fulfill the needs of the family and fill the back of our farm's pickup three or four times when the corn was ripe. We would then drive the pickup into town and park it on the west side of the town square, selling the sweetest corn on earth for twenty-five cents a dozen.

The taste of a homegrown tomato cannot be equaled by those corporate farms that nowadays must pick the tomato before it is ripe in order for it to be delivered to the supermarket before becoming spoiled. I get a kick out of those signs advertising vine-ripened tomatoes each time we visit the local supermarkets nowadays. I don't understand how a vine-ripened tomato can be so void of the sweet juice that I remember running down my chin each time I picked one of our farm's vine-ripened tomatoes, eating it right there on the spot.

In that storm cellar located underneath the family's farmhouse, we could store enough canned or sacked fruits and vegetables to last for the year.

The process of picking, bagging, canning, and freezing the garden's harvest was one that required three or four weeks. It was a labor of love fueled by our imagination's abilities to anticipate the wonderful flavors and many family meals that would result from the harvest provided by a loving God, who blessed our farm each year with a bountiful crop.

It was necessary to go to town so we could purchase the few items that we didn't produce on the farm. Some items like tissue and toilet paper, we gladly bought. If you have ever read about farmers using the pages from catalogs or corn husks then you may need to be set straight on the truth about farm toiletries. This may have been the practice dictated in years before I began my reign as a farm kid, but I can assure you that no one would prefer the corn cob to the squeezably soft stuff that comes from grocery store shelves nowadays.

I do recall many journeys to the famous one or two-hole outdoor toilets that city slickers believe are still in use today. It was a refreshing experience, especially in the dead of winter when the temperatures dipped below zero, and that nasty north wind found a way to blow up from the bottom of the already cold wooden throne.

The camaraderie that existed between the individual family farms was another important part of rural life that today seems to have been lost. A camaraderie that had families doing each others chores when vacations, illness, or other reasons made it necessary for travel away from the farm.

Whatever the reason, whether it was related to economics or health, the community of family farms was always quick to respond to the needs of any farm when a call for help arose.

Before the machinery was invented that would shell the corn off the cob in the field as it was picked, the corn-shelling equipment needed to remove the corn kernel from the cob was expensive and owned by very few. Those that did own a corn Sheller would each fall make the circuit around the farms in our district to shell corn off of the ear so that it could be placed into the corm dryers, the barn granary, or taken to town for sale at the local granary.

The help needed for this task at each farm would come from those families that lived on the farms that bordered the farm that was having its corn shelled. This was one of those unwritten rules that would help ensure that the job was done in an efficient manner, as the corn at each farm needed to be shelled before the winter storms hit.

The women would also come to each farm for the purpose of ensuring that no one went hungry. The meals provided at each stop on the corn-shelling circuit were legendary.

We kids always made sure we got involved in the corn-shelling act. My favorite activity was to stand next to the piles of picked field corn with shovel or pitch fork in hand, which I would use to exterminate any unfortunate rat or mouse that made a break for freedom as the corn pile got smaller and smaller.

As technology increased, so the camaraderie of the community farms in our area decreased as each farm eventually purchased the equipment needed to process the harvest within the decreasing time allotted, and each year the farms seemed to be getting bigger and bigger.

Without realizing it, each year farm kids received an education in the field of economics, lessons that increased in complexity each year due to the fast and ever-changing conditions that redefined the parameters dictating success or failure for each individual family farm.

I don't think we ever did pay off that brand-new tractor we had to buy in order to be able to farm our 180 acres plus the acreage that we ended up renting as we tried to make ends meet on our farm. That is, we did not pay it off until that day came when we sold the tractor as part of our going-out-of-the-family-farm-business sale.

I will never forget that day when my parents made the announcement to us kids that we would be moving from our farm to the capital city of our state, an announcement that had to be bitter for my dad, as I can only imagine how difficult it must have been for a man as proud as him to finally concede defeat in that battle of surviving the economic pitfalls of making a living on the farm.

Foolish teenager that I was, the idea of moving to the city was exciting and actually welcomed, as I figured that the amount of work required of me as a city kid during the year would drop off substantially.

This thought was proven foolish by the fact that while living in the capital city, I found myself each summer going back to the farm that my grandma and grandpa continued to try and operate, helping out with the summer duties. You see, living in the city was not only a confusing scenario full of silly rituals, it was boring!

And relating to those long-haired city kids was next to impossible. They viewed me as a hick from the sticks, I viewed them as hippies, and the summer escape to the farm was as much a relief to me as it probably was for my sisters to get rid of me for the summer.

The worst part for me was in leaving my best friend on the farm. Yogi was as much a part of me as any other member of our family. The day we loaded our furniture on the stock trailer and headed for the capital city is one I have successfully erased from memory. It was clear from his behavior that day that he knew something special was ending.

As I said, I was able to return each summer to work on the farm and play with my best friend. But he seemed to be aging faster than I was, and those adventures that we sought out in our youth seemed to be replaced with a desire to just sit together in the grass of a field and watch the clouds drift by.

As life has continued on for our family, those years on the farm have become more and more important to my own ability to survive life on this earth.

I now have an understanding of and great appreciation for how the trials and tribulations of growing up on the farm had indeed created the strength and resolve necessary for me to continue on past those roadblocks encountered in college and beyond.

The years on the farm were exactly what I needed in the process of developing a faith and resolve that would help me to persevere in the races that I choose to run today.

About the Author

John grew up on the family farm, and worked on his Uncles ranch, in the 1960's and early 70's. He left his home state of Nebraska at the age of twenty three to pursue a career in electronic engineering. After receiving a degree he spent twelve years in the avionic industry working in Arizona. While working in avionics, John met his wife Melissa.

John and Melissa then spent five years working in a family owned construction business, leaving it to work for a leading company in the gaming industry for thirteen years. During this time they had the pleasure to work and live in Nevada, Mississippi, Arizona and California.

They have also been fortunate to serve the Lord on three short term mission trips, in Cabo Frio, Brazil; Malindi, Kenya (East Africa), and Angra dos Heis, Brazil.

John has maintained the passion for fishing that he developed as a child, and that he talks about in his first book. He has enjoyed traveling in pursuit of the next catch, but will leave the writing about fishing for the experts.

John's best friend Yogi was irreplaceable, and John has not had a dog like him since. John and Melissa have developed an attachment to cats, although they don't really enjoy swimming as much as Yogi did.

Utilizing a compassion for people, and a desire to serve God, they hope to continue serving in a ministry that will help people to achieve the abundant life we where all created to live.

They have two daughters, and are currently living in Hawaii, where the fishing is really good.

This is John's first published book.

www.ingramcontent.com/pod-product-compliance
Lightning Source LLC
Chambersburg PA
CBHW030346290526
45785CB00004B/1626